PROTECTING AGAINST

ETERNAL

IDENTITY THEFT

REMEMBERING
YOUR DIVINE WORTH

PROTECTING AGAINST
ETERNAL
IDENTITY THEFT

BARBARA D. LOCKHART
WENDY C. TOP & BRENT L. TOP

Covenant Communications, Inc.

TABLE OF CONTENTS

WHO DO YOU THINK YOU ARE?

WE HEAR THIS QUESTION ALL too often in our lives, almost always in a negative context. More often than not it is expressed in a cutting, hurtful, rude, mean, or condescending way intended to "put us in our place." Even though the words may not be spoken, it shouts loudly, "You're not as good as you think you are!" or "You're not so special!" or "You're not entitled to any extraordinary privilege or treatment." You can almost hear the derision and feel the "bite" when you even think of the question, *Who do you think you are?* That's exactly what Satan wants you to think and feel. Because that's how *he* views your identity.

In contrast, the question takes on a totally different meaning when heard in a divine context. The Prophet Joseph Smith once remarked, "Would to God I could tell you who I am" (Orson F. Whitney, *Life of Heber C. Kimball* [Salt Lake City: Bookcraft, 1974], 222). While we do not know all that the Prophet meant by this statement, it is implicit that for him, as with all of us, there is more than "meets the eye." There is a spiritual—even divine—identity that each of us possesses that, though obscured by our mortal experience, if fully understood would heighten our self-respect and inspire us to a greater realization of our divine potential.

When viewed with spiritual understanding and eternal perspective, the question *Who do you think you are?* is the polar opposite of the way the world uses it. Satan puts down, but God lifts up. *Who do you think you are?* is God's loving invitation to better understand that "You are special!" and "You are infinitely more than you think you are!" and "You are entitled to special treatment and privileges." It is that message—understanding our true and eternal identity and the means used by the adversary to rob us of that imperative knowledge—that prompted this book.

The concept of a book to help God's children understand their eternal identity is Barbara Lockhart's "brainchild." A powerful personal experience kindled in her heart a sure testimony of God's perfect love. It was an experience that changed her forever. From that time, she has spent her life learning, relearning, and teaching others what it really means to be a child of God—a son or daughter of infinite worth and potential. She has collected ideas; read and conducted studies about perceptions of identity and self-worth; and dissected teachings of the scriptures, latter-day prophets, and apostles on the subject as well as the thoughts of other inspired writers and thinkers. Combining all of this with personal experiences and countless inspired insights of her own, Barbara devoted herself to helping her students at Brigham Young University come to know and feel the power of personal identity. Through teaching religious education classes at BYU, Barbara became acquainted with Brent, and they have had interesting gospel discussions through the years. Sharing the same passion for the gospel generally and the doctrine of eternal identity specifically, Wendy was brought into this collaborative effort and contributed her unique insights.

> This type of identity theft could be called the "spiritual crime of the ages."

The term *identity theft* is a relatively recent invention, although the practice undoubtedly predates the Internet. Although we primarily think of *identity theft* today in terms of financial fraud, there has long been another kind of "identity theft"—a spiritual fraud that creates even more problems and inflicts more pain. It could be characterized as the "spiritual crime of the ages." How do we protect ourselves from that? It is our hope that this book will convince you that it's even more important to protect your divine identity than it is to protect your financial identity.

If you have ever gone to the Internet to find information about a particular topic, you've probably found a site that addresses the topic with FAQs—frequently asked questions. That's how we've organized this book. Each chapter addresses a FAQ concerning our true identity and Satan's efforts to rob us of that identity. Even if you haven't thought to ask some of the questions posed in these chapters, hopefully they will stimulate other questions and lead to important insights as to who you are, where you came from, why you are here, what your eternal destiny is, and how you can achieve it.

This book is both doctrinal and practical. It is a spiritual self-help book in the truest sense of the word. We believe, as President Boyd K. Packer has so often taught, that teaching doctrine is a much more powerful and permanent way to improve behavior than is the teaching of behavior (see *Mine Errand from the Lord* [Salt Lake City: Deseret Book Company, 2008], 307). Understanding the doctrine of eternal worth and identity will also provide practical application through the Spirit. We don't have to give you a list of all the "dos" and "don'ts" to protect yourself from eternal identity theft. You will, however, find in each chapter important teachings from prophets and apostles that hopefully will stimulate a sort of "identity check." Each chapter also includes "Belief Windows," questions to ask yourself about your own belief system and how you view yourself. As you learn or relearn these fundamental teachings, ponder your own beliefs and feelings, and open your heart with righteous desires, the Spirit of God will help you make the necessary applications and/or course corrections in your life. In this way doctrine combined with personal inspiration leads to spiritual solutions. That is the kind of self-help the Lord desires for us all.

We alone are responsible for the applications and ideas presented in this book. They do not represent official doctrine or the authorized position of The Church of Jesus Christ of Latter-day Saints. Therefore, we recognize (and hope you will as well) that we do not declare doctrine. We have sought to ensure that the teachings contained herein are in harmony with those doctrines by using the standard works and statements from the Brethren, but if there are errors or doctrinal deficiencies, they are ours and ours alone.

What Is Identity Theft?

THE TERM *IDENTITY THEFT* HAS become so common in the last ten years that we now see or hear it on a daily basis. "Identity theft case puts 130 million at risk" declares one headline. An ad on a web site announces "ID Theft Recovery—Get your identity back now—Stop being a victim." Television advertisers feature distraught victims recounting the cost of identity theft in their personal and financial affairs in hopes that frightened viewers will put out money to be protected from this epidemic crime. We are continually warned in our private and public financial correspondence to be aware of some new identity theft scam.

Identity theft has now become a fact of our modern technology-infused life. Information on important steps to protect our identity is readily available everywhere, yet identity theft persists. Interestingly, one information site declares that identity theft is a misnomer: No one can steal your *identity*; they can only *use* your personal information to steal money, goods, and other things that may rightfully belong to you or others. You still know who you are and you keep and use your own identity. Perhaps "personal information theft" would be a more accurate description.

However, one type of very real identity theft occurs on a much more serious level, causing untold destruction to the human soul. This book discusses this kind of identity theft—eternal identity theft. But just as with "personal information" identity theft, no one can actually steal your eternal identity, either. No one and nothing can alter who you *really* are. Yet, more insidiously than with personal information theft, what *can* be stolen is your knowledge, fulfillment, and enjoyment of your true, eternal identity. Knowing your true, divine identity is crucial to your success. As President Dieter F. Uchtdorf has testified, each of us is more glorious than we can possibly imagine—each of us is divine. And the knowledge of that divinity, he says, changes everything (see "The Reflection in the Water," CES Fireside for Young Adults, Brigham Young University, Nov. 1, 2009).

Because the knowledge of our divinity changes us forever, Satan will use whatever he can—deception, distortion, distraction, dissatisfaction, exhaustion, manipulation, pacification, obstruction, and a myriad of other things—to keep us from realizing our divine nature. He wants us to forget, ignore, misunderstand, underestimate, reject, or even rebel against our divine identity.

This type of identity theft has existed since before time began. Even in the premortal life, a third of our brothers and sisters succumbed to Satan's wiles. The eternal toll such theft has taken and is taking on Heavenly Father's children is far greater than all of the physical, emotional, and spiritual damage that could possibly be done under the current plague of personal information theft.

The Threat to Our Eternal Identity

Satan and his minions, all of whom have eternally rejected their divine identity, are ruthlessly bent on keeping us from understanding and realizing ours. Why are we vulnerable to these attempts at stealing our identity? To begin with, we come into this life with a spiritual amnesia about our true origins. We must walk by faith—and while we're doing that, Satan knows exactly who we are and the power and majesty we possess! From the moment we are born on this earth, it takes faith in Christ to rediscover who we are, why we are here, and where we are going after this life. It is a challenge that is meant to teach and test us, and we can be sure that Satan will take advantage of that. It is his last opportunity to exercise his power—and he will stop at nothing. We can't be foolish enough to think that he will ever show any mercy. We can't be too careful.

Furthermore, this kind of identity theft may affect every aspect of our being. There is no part of us that is immune to Satan's pressures and influences: spiritual, emotional, mental, physical, and social. They are all tied together in the human soul. Now that we have had the privilege of coming to earth and have been given the gift of a body, it is impossible to affect the spirit or other aspects of our being without it having an impact on the body and vice versa. Body and spirit will shape each other forever. Indeed, the Doctrine and Covenants teaches us clearly that the spirit and the body together are the *soul* of man (see D&C 88:15).

Symptoms of Eternal Identity Theft

Because losing sight of our divine identity affects every aspect of our existence, it can wreak havoc with our lives and be very debilitating. How do we recognize eternal identity theft in our own life? Here are just a few of the symptoms of identity theft:

- Feeling as if we can never do enough or be good enough
- Feeling alone or unloved
- Being motivated by fear instead of faith
- Not liking our bodies
- Thinking we cannot be forgiven, cannot progress, or cannot be saved
- Feeling pressure to perfect ourselves and do it now
- Thinking we have to earn God's love
- Thinking our worth is dependent on the way we look or the things we do
- Trying to succeed without God's help
- Thinking happiness comes from pleasing others or self-gratification
- Feeling overwhelmed by life and its trials
- Letting other people decide our identity and value
- Spiritual emptiness and longing
- Feeling constant guilt
- Feeling that life is not fair
- Ingratitude
- Feeling we are not as good as others or that we are better than others
- Not understanding our total dependence on the Atonement of Christ

As you consider the above list, you may think of additional maladies that are linked to a misunderstanding or underappreciation of divine identity. There are countless ways that identity theft can damage us, including many that are unique to each individual. Consider the ills that continually plague your own life and how they could be improved or even healed if you could see more clearly and know more certainly that you are the very offspring of God—if you could trust that He desires to redeem you, personally, through His Son Jesus Christ no matter who you are.

There are many examples in the scriptures of people who have wandered away and fallen into Satan's traps but who were reclaimed through our Savior, Jesus Christ. Symbolically, the parable of the prodigal son (see Luke 15:11–32) represents not only those who have fallen into flagrant sin but, on another level, all of us because we "all have sinned, and come short of the glory of God" (Rom. 3:23). After taking his inheritance and squandering it, the younger of the two sons in this parable came to his senses and decided to return to his father. "I will arise and go to my father, and will say unto him, Father, I have sinned against heaven, and before thee, and am no more worthy to be called thy son: make me as one of thy hired servants" (Luke 15:18, 19).

Instead, the father, upon seeing again his beloved son whom he thought was dead, called forth the best celebration possible—not a celebration for a hired servant, but a feast befitting a beloved son. "Bring forth the best robe, and put it on him [distinction]; and put a ring on his hand [a sign of authority], and shoes on his feet [slaves or servants went barefoot]: and bring hither the fatted calf [a great sacrifice of resources saved only for the most joyous family occasions], and kill it; and let us eat and be merry: for this my son was dead, and is alive again; he was lost, and is found" (Luke 15:22–24).

The father's joy was indescribable, and his love and his blessings knew no bounds—his son was lost and now was found! Of course the son was always his father's child, but he thought that he had forfeited his identity, inheritance, and position in the family. Yet he discovered or re-discovered, as we can, that there is always hope in Christ if we desire to reclaim that

Our Savior has paid the price to redeem us from the slavery of sin and restore us to our true identity.

which was lost. Our Savior has paid the price to redeem us from the slavery of sin and restore us to our true identity—to our rightful place in His Father's royal and godly family (see Rom. 8:15–17).

God expresses in these magnificent words from the Doctrine and Covenants His great joy when we remember who we are and return to Him: "Remember, the worth of souls is great in the sight of God; For behold, the Lord your Redeemer has suffered death in the flesh; wherefore he suffered the pain of all men, that all men might repent and come unto him. And he hath risen again from the dead, that he might bring all men unto him, on conditions of repentance. And how great is his joy in the soul that repenteth!" (D&C 18:10–13).

Barbara experienced how coming to this knowledge of her divine nature changed everything. She had succumbed for many years to eternal identity theft and eventually was rescued from it by Heavenly Father. She describes it this way: "For no apparent reason, as a young teenager, I began to greatly dislike myself. For nearly fifteen years, I victimized myself with terribly negative self-talk. In the process, I doubted that my life had any real purpose or value. Thinking that maybe achieving success in school, music, and sports would allow me to have good self-esteem, I was driven to succeed. Succeed I did, but no change occurred in my negative feelings about myself. It wasn't until my early thirties when I soulfully plead with Heavenly Father that the negative self-talk ceased. Heavenly Father blessed me to know that He loves me and that my life does have purpose and value. He changed me so I could feel deep in my heart that I am precious to Him and could feel grateful for who I am. This change came by the Spirit rather than through anything I could do on my own. My desire is to share this testimony because of the enormous joy, peace, and purpose it has given me. It truly has changed everything for the good."

In this book, we hope to show how each one of us, like the prodigal son, must "come to ourselves" and remember our divine identity, strengthen our faith in Christ, and seek protection and cover from the unrelenting influence of Satan that may blind us to our true power and destiny. Let us emphasize again that this is a challenging process that takes sincere faith in the Savior. We need to be gentle with ourselves and realize what we are up against. Although it may be tempting, there is no point in being frustrated or discouraged as we engage in the process to either help ourselves or others. Frustration and discouragement are part of Satan's arsenal, not the Lord's. It is worth all our best efforts to find the precious pearl that is our true identity and prepare ourselves to receive again the royal robes that we left behind in our heavenly home.

Protection against Identity Theft

The gospel of Jesus Christ—specifically His Atonement—is the best insurance to protect us from divine identity theft. Seeking the power that comes with understanding and applying the doctrines of the gospel, the intention of this book is to identify, warn about, and urge protection against identity theft of the soul—spirit and body. We hope to join hands with you, our fellow travelers on this journey, and become more aware of the terrible dangers that surround us and learn how to avoid them.

The Lord wants us to remember who we really are, to recognize those things in mortality that are cleverly disguised traps, and to recognize those things that are real and eternal. Coming to a deeper understanding of our divine identity is definitely possible with a greater understanding of the meaning and power of the Atonement and how to apply it in every detail of our lives.

Christ is our guide and our rescuer in all respects of everything we are and everything we experience. This is true not only in mortality but throughout our entire journey in the plan of salvation. Learning of Him and His infinitely compassionate, saving doctrines and sacrifice can help us learn who we are. Losing ourselves in search of Him will help us find ourselves. Seeking His way instead of the world's way will save us unnecessary trials and suffering. Finding and believing the truth about who we are will make life richer, fuller, and certainly much happier.

Christ said, "I am come that they might have life, and that they might have it more abundantly" (John 10:10). Eternal identity theft robs us of the abundant life we are meant to live both here and hereafter. With identity theft of our real selves, as with anything else that we encounter in this world, Jesus Christ is the only true answer. The one and only way to find our true selves is to find Christ first.

Test Your Belief Window

What we believe about ourselves determines our outlook on life and also our actions. The *belief window* is a lens through which we see life, much like glasses. Franklin Covey, a provider of time management training and assessment services for organizations and individuals (largely founded on the work of Dr. Stephen R. Covey, author of *Seven Habits of Highly Effective People*), teaches that every person has a belief window. Ideally, we would understand the truth of all things and therefore through our belief window we would see "things as they really are." If our belief window has been tampered

> "Each of us sees the world through our belief window. The beliefs that we have are the lenses of reality for each of us."
>
> —*Connie Blakemore, BYU Devotional, July 28, 1998*

with, as happens with divine identity theft, we hear the truth but then distort it by filtering it through our erroneous belief window. It is like wearing glasses that are the wrong prescription.

As an example of that distortion, a prophet may testify that Heavenly Father loves each of us. If you believe that you are not loved or that no one can love you, you *hear* the prophet's *words*, but rather than believe his message, you think something different. You may say to yourself, *God does love His children, but He does not love me.* You may be convinced that God cannot love you because of something you have done or because you are "different." Therefore, even though you hear the truth from the prophet, your errant belief window does not allow you to incorporate that truth into your life and see things "as they really are" (Jacob 4:13).

> ## Belief Window
>
> What are your personal beliefs about yourself— your spirit, your body, your purpose, your standing before the Lord?
>
> Who are you?

If your belief window is accurate, on the other hand, when you hear the prophet testify that Heavenly Father loves each of us with a perfect love, the Holy Ghost will testify to your spirit that this is true. That truth then becomes a very real part of you. You will feel Heavenly Father's love for you and feel the peace that accompanies His love—a key component to understanding your divine identity.

As you read this book, think about your belief window regarding each particular idea. Remember that *your* belief window greatly affects how you will interpret and incorporate the message. You can trust that we will do our best to teach only that which is true. Divine truth inspires and strengthens. If you do not feel bolstered by the truths discussed, examine your belief window to see if it has been distorted. Your belief window may influence you to misunderstand what is being taught, but if influenced by the Spirit, your belief window will clear and enable you to see "things as they really are."

You may want to reread some pages to reinforce your understanding of your identity after the Spirit has helped you "clean" your window. Understanding your identity will stave off much of the harm the adversary seeks to inflict on you. Knowing and maintaining your divine identity enables you to live a hopeful and a happy life even in the midst of tribulation. President Thomas S. Monson has promised that great blessings are in store for us in spite of the storm clouds gathering about us, and these blessings are beyond measure. He maintained that with faith in Christ there is nothing in the world that can defeat us, as the future is as bright as our faith (see "Be of Good Cheer," *Ensign*, May 2009).

As you seek to know your Heavenly Father and yourself as His crowning creation, the Holy Ghost will reveal to you who you really are.

What Is My True Eternal Identity?

With the restored gospel of Jesus Christ comes not only an understanding of "*things* as they really are" (Jacob 4:13, emphasis added), but also *who* we really are. What an incredible blessing it is that we are given to know where we came from, why we are here, where we are going, and what our ultimate destiny is. The gospel teaches us the reality of life so we do not have to worry about or be confused as to what life is all about. We know life as it really is . . . amazing!

As we gain a deeper understanding and appreciation of who we are, we gain an optimistic perspective on life and particularly the individual life we have been given. We realize day in and day out that we are eternal beings who, right now, are living in mortality, our second and temporary estate. C. S. Lewis has written that no one has ever met a mere mortal because we are all immortal beings (see *The Weight of Glory* [New York: HarperCollins, 2001]). Mortality definitely does not define us. We truly are the offspring of God (even two-year-olds and teenagers!).

> **Identity Check**
>
> "I believe and testify that our spirits are special spirits and were reserved until this generation to stand strong against the evil winds that blow, and to stand straight and upright with the heavy burdens that will be placed on us."
>
> —President James E. Faust, "The Voice of the Spirit," *Ensign*, April 1994, 10

Children of God

There is much about our existence prior to being born as spirit children of Heavenly Father that has not been revealed, yet Heavenly Father reveals to us through His prophets all the knowledge that is crucial to our eternal salvation. What we *do* know is that there is something about us that has always existed. There is no beginning and no end to our immortal being. In essence, and literally, there is something about our divine identity that is coeternal with God. The Prophet Joseph Smith revealed this remarkable truth:

> I am referring to . . . the soul, the mind of man, the immortal spirit. All men say God created it in the beginning. The very idea lessens man in my estimation. I do not believe the doctrine; I know better. . . . I am going to tell of things more noble.
>
> Intelligence exists upon a self-existent principle; it is a spirit from age to age, and there is no creation about it. . . .
>
> The first principles of man are self-existent with God. God found himself in the midst of spirits and glory, and because he was greater, he saw proper to institute laws whereby the rest could have the privilege of advancing like himself— that they might have one glory upon another and all the knowledge, power, and glory necessary to save the world of spirits. (*History of the Church*, 6:310–312.)

In some remarkable way that we do not yet fully understand, His great love for us motivated our Heavenly Father to provide us the opportunity to be born as His spirit children and thus begin our participation in an eternal plan of salvation that potentially may result in our becoming an exalted god like Him.

At the September 1995 general Relief Society meeting, we were given greater insight into our premortal identity by the First Presidency and Council of the Twelve Apostles in *The Family: A Proclamation to the World*. Through the proclamation we are told that our gender is an essential part of our eternity identity, and that it has always been so; we are also told that each of us, men and women alike, is a beloved spirit child of heavenly parents, created in the image of God, and that we each have a divine destiny. The New Testament tells us that "we are the children of God: and if children, then heirs; heirs of God, and joint-heirs with Christ" (Rom. 8:16–17). As heirs, we inherit Their legacy, possessions, power, and position, and we also inherit our identity from Them.

We know through modern revelation that our spirits are composed of matter, just as God's is, though it is so pure and refined as to be invisible to the human eye (see D&C 131:7, 8). Surely it must be that the spirit matter that makes up our spirit bodies literally contains Their "divine DNA" (for lack of a better way of describing it) or its spiritual counterpart. "An intelligent being, in the image of God," Elder Parley P. Pratt wrote, "possesses every organ, attribute, sense, sympathy, affection, of will, wisdom, love, power and gift, which is possessed by God himself. . . . These attributes are in embryo, and are to be gradually developed" (*Key to Theology* [Salt Lake City: Deseret News Printers and Publishers, 1915], 96–97). Prophetic statements such as these give us all the more reason to trust in and identify with the reality of our divine nature. This is who we were before we ever came to earth. This is who we continue to be even now. We can reject or rebel against our identity, but that doesn't alter the fact: both our origins and our potential are divine.

> ### Identity Check
>
> "I want to tell you, each and every one of you, that you are well acquainted with God our heavenly Father, or the great Elohim. You are all well acquainted with Him, for there is not a soul of you but what has lived in His house and dwelt with Him year after year. . . . There is not a person here today but what is a son or a daughter of that Being. In the spirit world their spirits were first begotten and brought forth, and they lived there with their parents for ages before they came here. This, perhaps, is hard for many to believe, but it is the greatest nonsense in the world not to believe it."
>
> —President Brigham Young, *Journal of Discourses,* 4:216

With a divine origin comes a royal birthright. Our Father in Heaven is not only God but also a king and high priest—King of all creation and the Source of all power in heaven and earth. We have the opportunity and ability through the Atonement of Christ to inherit not only the titles and privileges of kings and queens, priests and priestesses, but the attendant powers as well. Whether we recognize it or not, each one of us is thus royalty, a prince or a princess in the eyes of our Heavenly Father and our Savior. That royalty is part of our present-day divine inheritance. Someday, however, if we live, as President Harold B. Lee said, "loyal to the royal within us" we will no longer be merely princesses and princes, but rather as "joint-heirs" with the Lord we will become truly kings and queens and priests and priestesses (see "Be Loyal to the Royal Within You," *Speeches of the Year, 1973*, Provo, UT: Brigham Young University Press, 1973). That is our royal destiny.

As children of Heavenly Parents, we are loved with a perfect love.

The scriptures teach us that God is love (see 1 John 4:8). Thus, as children of Heavenly Parents—the very eternal embodiments of divine love—we are loved with a perfect love and carry with us in our very natures divine love. This is part of our eternal identity—a divine reality impossible to change. There is no power or influence that can ever diminish God's perfect and everlasting love for each one of us. After teaching that we are children of God and joint-heirs with Christ, the Apostle Paul assured the Saints, "For I am persuaded, that neither death, nor life, nor angels, nor principalities, nor powers, nor things present, nor things to come, Nor height, nor depth, nor any other creature, shall be able to separate us from the love of God, which is in Christ Jesus our Lord" (Rom. 8:38–39). Only we, by our own choices, desires, and distorted beliefs about our eternal identity, allow Satan to interfere with our ability to know this love.

The Plan and Preparation for Our Happiness

In our premortal home we were tenderly nurtured by Heavenly Parents with the understanding that we were expected to one day become like Them and take our rightful place in Their kingdom. Yet, they had perfect respect for our individual identity and the eternal law of agency. Forcing us was not only out of the question, it was impossible. We can't be forced to be truly righteous—to become like our perfect Parents. So the plan of salvation was instituted that would make it possible for us to return to Them by our own choice, even if we chose badly or made mistakes. For eons of time all of Heavenly Father's children were thoroughly taught the principles of the gospel and that through Christ, the Firstborn of our Father's children, we could overcome all of the effects of our mortal experience that would keep us from returning home, if we followed Him.

The plan could not have worked with anyone other than Jesus Christ, the Sinless One, as the Savior. Yet Lucifer, our adversary, "rebelled against the Only Begotten Son whom the Father loved and who was in the bosom of the Father" (D&C 76:25). He tried desperately to steal our identity as heirs to the throne and individual agents with the right to choose our own destiny. He sought to convince us that he could save every one of us if we would all surrender our agency, individuality, and divine potential to him. (Perhaps he accused Christ of not loving us enough to save *all* of us!)

As intelligent spirit children, we had the privilege to stand up for Christ or to follow Satan. We, unlike those who followed Satan, genuinely exercised faith in the Father's plan. We believed in our Savior, trusted in His perfect love, and believed that He really would indeed

> # We had faith that Christ could save us no matter what we experienced in mortality.

fulfill the exacting requirements of an infinite and eternal Atonement and that it would have the power to exalt us. We had faith that He could save us no matter what we experienced in mortality. We knew that it would not be easy but that only our Savior was willing to pay the ultimate price to assure us the freedom to choose, the freedom to fulfill our destinies. We have no idea how long this war of faith and ideas raged, but eventually our testimonies of Christ's Atonement grew increasingly more powerful until we conquered Satan (see Rev. 12:11).

It is further evidence of the great love of God and Christ for us that the Atonement wiped away our sins in the premortal realm and mitigated the effects of Adam's transgression so that we could be completely innocent and free to choose again in our infant mortal state (see D&C 93:38). It also allows us to maintain our innocence on this earth until we have sufficiently learned right from wrong and begin to become accountable. How merciful and loving is the Lord!

All of this is made possible through the sufferings of Christ, so that when we arrive in this life we are free to fulfill our destiny through our own choices! Lehi taught us that "men are free according to the flesh; *and all things are given them which are expedient unto man*. And they are free to choose liberty and eternal life, through the great Mediator of all men, or to choose captivity and death, according to the captivity and power of the devil; for he seeketh that all men might be miserable like unto himself" (2 Ne. 2:27; emphasis added). Though we exercised faith in Christ's Atonement before, the Lord will never force us to accept His Atonement here on earth. His reverent respect for the agency of every single individual is one of the greatest tokens of His love. It is easy to respect agency when it is used wisely, but when it is misused it takes a perfect love and respect to not step in and take it away. Just ask the parents of wayward children!

Yet even more was done to prepare the faithful for earth life. Elder Bruce R. McConkie explained that Heavenly Father's way of helping us to continue our diligence and to remain on the path toward exaltation was to send us to earth through the lineage of Abraham and Jacob, the house of Israel. "Members of the Church were foreordained to be saved in the celestial kingdom; they were chosen in the pre-existence to gain eternal life" (*Doctrinal New Testament Commentary* [Salt Lake City: Deseret Book Company, 2002], 2:274; see also 3:64).

Belief Window

Do you believe that *you* were foreordained to eternal life?

If not, why not?

While we were also foreordained to come to earth at certain times in certain lands with certain missions and callings, our foreordinations to the house of Israel were the most important. Being foreordained to this ultimate blessing meant that we were "among the noble and great ones" that Abraham saw (see Abr. 3:22) and we are chosen to one day rule and reign with God in the house of Israel forever. The Lord had faith in us and knew that we could succeed. That doesn't mean that we automatically receive this privilege, but that because of our obedience and love for the Lord greater opportunities and blessings were given to bring it about. It also means that we have greater responsibility to lead others to eternal life (see Abr. 3:23, D&C 133:32–34). Likewise, it doesn't mean that those who were not foreordained can never receive eternal life!

Thus, we were equipped with those things we would need to be successful here on earth. In addition to being taught the plan of salvation, exercising faith in the Atonement, and being foreordained for exaltation because of our faithfulness, we were promised potent tools that would help us have power over Satan, accomplish our mission here on earth, and return to our royal parents.

Each of us has been given the Light of Christ to help us discern between right and wrong, believe in Christ, and do good (see Moroni 7:12–18).

Those who were foreordained to eternal life and who take upon themselves the covenant of baptism receive an even greater gift: the consummate gift of the Holy Ghost—the guidance, protection and even presence of God available as we are worthy. But God's promises of help and protection don't stop there. He ordained prophets who speak His words and give instructions to His children while they are on earth. Those prophets speak and record the words of the Lord and provide us with holy scriptures from which we can daily—even hourly—consult and draw strength and direction. Through priesthood power—God's actual power delegated to man—we can access His power in our personal lives for protection, healing, guidance, and more. And of course, on top of all of this He grants us the supernal gift of communicating with Him intimately in constant prayer. He gives us all of this and more individualized blessings as well. We are covered, surrounded, protected, and infused with every tool and guide we need if we desire them. What more could we possibly ask?

Identity Check

"We humble people, who feel ourselves sometimes so worthless, so good-for-nothing, we are not so worthless as we think. There is not one of us that he has not cared for and caressed. There is not one of us that He has not desired to save and that He has not devised means to save. There is not one of us that he has not given his angels charge concerning. We may be insignificant and contemptible in our own eyes and in the eyes of others, but the truth remains that we are the children of God and that He has actually given His angels—invisible beings of power and might—charge concerning us, and they watch over us and have us in their keeping."

—George Q. Cannon, *Gospel Truth*, Jerrold L. Newquist, comp. (Salt Lake City: Deseret Book, 1987), 1:2

And yet, there is more! Through God's priesthood, the Church has been organized according to His divine pattern to care for, help prepare and perfect those who choose to participate. He has instituted covenants and ordinances that help to mark our path, bind us to Him, and keep us in the way of eternal life as we accept and live them. When we visit His holy temple we can renew our strength, more fully understand our mission on earth, see more clearly our divine identity, and learn what we must do to prepare for our eternal destiny. In that sacred place, those who have accepted the Atonement of Christ find the ordinances and instructions that reveal the sacred symbolic knowledge we must possess to enter into our Father's kingdom. Only there do we learn how to be kings and queens, priests and priestesses, gods and goddesses. Our Father and Savior have laid out a clear path with constant help along the way.

The Lord has done all of this and more for us because of His exquisite love for us and His desire that we should return to Him and know what He knows, love as He loves, and experience what He experiences. How true are the words of one of those prophets He sent to us, President Ezra Taft Benson, who said, "God loves us. He's watching us, he wants us to succeed, and we'll know someday that he has not left one thing undone for the eternal welfare of each of us" ("Insights: We Seek That Which Is Praiseworthy," *Ensign*, July 1975, 62–63).

The Great Gift

There is one more extremely important gift that manifests God's incomparable love to us. To fully appreciate it, we must consider the influence of Satan upon those who were cast out. The adversary began his efforts at divine identity theft eons ago. Even though all spirits born to our Heavenly Parents are divine in nature, Satan was able to influence "a third part of the hosts of heaven" (D&C 29:36)—a substantial number—to reject their identity. Tragically, they were cast out with him and lost forever.

Just as people fall for get-rich-quick scams today, these spirits may have initially believed the scam Lucifer presented to them. In a get-rich-quick scam, disreputable people convince you to give them your money with the guarantee of a sizeable return on your investment—without you having to do a thing. You trust these people to make you rich. But they take your money with no concern for you and no intent to ever give you any money back. Lucifer guaranteed salvation to spirits who didn't need to do a thing other than trust him. Lucifer did this with no love for those spirits and no intention to help them progress. Like mortal scammers,

Lucifer could never have delivered on his too-good-to-be-true promises because those promises were in opposition to eternal law.

However, God's love for his children is so great that He would never impose such an ultimate punishment on them simply for being deceived. Only their eventual complete rebellion and rejection of the Father, His Only Begotten Son, the love that motivated Them, and Their eternal plan of salvation could bring about the awful consequences that occurred. They refused God's great gift, and He could not help them. Instead of progressing and receiving at least some level of salvation, as will all of those born on earth (except the few sons of perdition), these spirits forfeited any hope of happiness or progression.

As Lucifer and those who went with him were cast out, they endured the greatest punishment possible. President Joseph Fielding Smith said, "The greatest punishment ever given was proclaimed against Lucifer and his angels. To be denied the privilege of mortal bodies forever is the greatest curse of all. These spirits have no progression, no hope of resurrection and eternal life. Doomed are they to eternal misery" (*Conference Report*, October 1965, 28). No wonder "the Heavens wept over [them]" (D&C 76:26).

We know that we on earth chose Christ because we continued in our progression from the first estate and were blessed to enter this second estate. We were not deceived by Satan in our first estate and thus did not succumb to his attempts there to rob us of our identity. As we entered mortality, we were given the next great divine gift of love: a body that will one day become ours forever, immortalized and glorified according to the glory we are willing to receive (see D&C 88:22). It was not designed to be a mere physical object to be used as we see fit but a sacred temple of our Father, to house our divine spirit and to receive His Spirit. Like our spirit, it has the capacity, again through the Atonement of Christ, to one day become celestial like God's. With the addition of a physical body, though temporarily mortal, we became immortal souls.

> **Belief Window**
>
> When you think of your own identity, do you think of your immortal self as both body and spirit together?
>
> Do you think of both as a token of God's love?

The Body and the Spirit Are the Soul of Man

The Lord defines the soul in D&C 88:15: "And the spirit and the body are the soul of man." In this second estate, our eternal identity has thus been expanded. Elder David A. Bednar explained that our spirit and body make up our identity (see "Things as They Really Are," *Brigham Young University 2009–2010 Devotional and Fireside Speeches*, May 2009, 2).

Your body is an essential aspect of your identity now and for eternity. Now that we are souls with a body and a spirit, we are more like our Heavenly Father and Savior than we were as spirits alone. Elder James E. Talmage proclaimed that "we have been taught . . . to look upon these bodies of ours as gifts from God. We regard [the body] as the sign of our royal birthright" (*Conference Report*, October 1913, 117). Thus, our body is not only a sacred gift and trust, but a token of our Heavenly Father's great love and a promise of future blessings.

Our Turn on Earth

So here we are! And who are we? Royal, divine gods and goddesses in training, clothed in holy temples of flesh and bones, living in a temporary, testing existence lovingly crafted by our Father for our benefit and progression. In spite of the fact that all we are and all we have come from Him, He allows us this opportunity to choose or reject what He has in store for us. President Ezra Taft Benson summed up this identity and our purpose here on earth so beautifully when he said:

> A few years ago, we knew our Elder Brother and our Father in heaven well. We rejoiced at the upcoming opportunity for earth life that could make it possible for us to have a fullness of joy like they had. We could hardly wait to demonstrate to our Father and our Brother, the Lord, how much we loved them and how we would be obedient to them in spite of the earthly opposition of the evil one.
>
> And now we're here—our memories are veiled—and we're showing God and ourselves what we can do. And

nothing is going to startle us more when we pass through the veil to the other side than to realize how well we know our Father and how familiar his face is to us.

. . . If we only knew it, there are heavenly hosts pulling for us—friends in heaven that we can't remember now, who yearn for our victory. This is our day to show what we can do—what life and sacrifice we can daily, hourly, instantly bring to God. If we give our all, we will get his all from the greatest of all. ("Insights: We Seek That Which Is Praiseworthy," *Ensign*, July 1975, 62–63.)

Understanding the divine nature of our being is one of the greatest blessings we can enjoy on this earth. Opening a deeper understanding of our eternal divine nature will allow us to fill the measure of our creation, because we see ourselves "as we really are." We will enjoy a stronger sense of purpose and a greater unity with Heavenly Father and His will for us as we embrace our divine identity. We will position ourselves to be blessed by the atoning sacrifice of Jesus Christ, to be purified, sanctified, and prepared to enjoy the blessings of eternity.

How Is Pride the Greatest Threat to My Identity?

BECAUSE OF THE VEIL OF forgetfulness that is mercifully draped over our minds as we enter this world, it is easy to understand how we can begin to think that this world is all that is real and that whatever we are here is all that we can ever be. As a result, we may find ourselves playing to the wrong audience.

Imagine an acclaimed actor in a popular play. This actor becomes so completely absorbed in playing his assigned role and becoming his temporary character that he begins to think like that character would think. He comes then to believe that the set, the props, the actors, the audience, and the plot are his real life and nothing else matters. He almost completely forgets his offstage identity. He lives for the applause and approval of the audience and his fellow actors. It is his only fulfillment. Yet, one day the play will end, the curtains will close for the last time, and the realistic

> One day the veil of forgetfulness will be rolled back, and we will see that this life was a temporary role assignment, not our permanent identity.

but illusory set will be taken down or used for other plays. The stage will suddenly be empty and the other players will have moved on.

Will the actor have exchanged his true and real identity for a transitory false one that will one day vanish and leave him empty? This may happen to us during our time in this temporary world if we do not keep our minds and our energies focused on what is real. One day the curtains of heaven will, conversely, be opened, the veil of forgetfulness will be rolled back, and we will see and remember that this life was a temporary role assignment, not our permanent identity. So while we will each take on many different roles and challenges in this life, our eternal worth and identity remain unchanged. As mentioned previously, the question is whether we will rediscover and embrace them.

What Is Real in This Life?

Because it is so easy to be beguiled and overcome by the artificial environment Satan creates on the earth, we must exercise great faith to remember who we are and see "things as they really are." Elder Richard G. Scott once shared a disturbing dream he had about Satan's attempts to literally steal his eternal identity. In his dream, he had been separated from his wife, and the throngs of people he encountered told him she was no longer the person he remembered. In fact, they told him, he himself was not the same. They were convincing in their insistence that soon he would not be able to remember his wife, his children, or his other loved ones. He was horrified.

Finally, he realized that those who surrounded him and were trying to convince him of their warped perspective were evil individuals who were lonely, unhappy individuals who wanted others to be equally lonely and unhappy. Only after he exercised unfailing faith was he able to see the reality of his situation and overcome the evil influences around him. Upon awakening from his dream he felt profound gratitude for Heavenly Father's plan and the reality that he would never lose his identity (see "Finding Happiness," *Brigham Young University 1996–1997 Devotional and Fireside Speeches* [Provo, UT: Brigham Young University, 1997]).

Lehi's Reality

How do we know what is real in the midst of this temporary test—this "hour upon the stage," as Shakespeare called earth life? How do we sort out our true identity in the midst of so many conflicting choices and vehement voices? Remember all of the tools our Heavenly parents gave us to help us find our way back to Them? This is where those things come in—prophets, scriptures, the Holy Ghost, prayer, families, the Church organization, the priesthood, ordinances, and, most of all, the temple. One of the most accurate portrayals of the realities of earth life comes from the prophet

Lehi through a dream (see 1 Ne. 8, 11–12). Though the truths contained therein were represented by symbols, the true states of earth life as seen by our Heavenly Father and Savior are absolutely real eternal verities. While we can't look around us and see mists of darkness, people clinging to an iron rod, a tree with brilliant white fruit, proud and extravagantly dressed people in a huge building with no foundation, or evil people falling into a river of filthy water, we *can* look around and see lost souls whose minds are blinded to the truths of who they are. We can see people who care only about being rich and powerful—proud and rebellious people who mock and intimidate the humble and righteous, and others who are just totally given over to wallowing in evil. We also see a very few who are

> While we can't look around us and see what Lehi saw in his dream, we *can* see lost souls whose minds are blinded to the truths of who they really are.

trying to serve the Lord in spite of the relentless pressure all around them to give in to sin. If we care to, we can even see the love such beings have for each other and the joy and peace they experience. Perhaps life would be easier if we saw it more in terms of Lehi's dream, so let's examine it and try to understand more clearly the reality of mortality.

After travelling in darkness for many hours and then pleading with the Lord for help, Lehi finds himself in a large and spacious field, interpreted as the world, just as we at birth find ourselves in the big, strange world, wide open with choices. In the midst of that field Lehi finds the tree of life (Jesus Christ and His Atonement), just as we have found the joy and blessings of the Atonement of Christ and His restored gospel. Lehi partakes of the marvelous fruit (the love of God), and it brings him such exquisite joy that he desires above all that his family partake with him, a blessing that we also naturally desire for others whom we truly love. If you are reading this book, you have probably experienced these same joys Lehi experienced. They are real—more real and powerful than anything on earth! They make the things of the world seem fleeting and futile by comparison.

Shown his father's dream, Nephi also sees its interpretation and how it plays out in real life. He understands the meaning of the tree of life and its delicious and desirable fruit when he is shown the reality of the condescension of God—Christ's Atonement, His mission to earth, and the multitudes who are blessed and healed by Him physically and spiritually (see 1 Ne. 11:13–31). He sees how the people in the great and spacious building are like the people who scorn, persecute, and murder the Lord, His Apostles, and His Saints because of their great pride in themselves (see 1 Ne. 11:32–35). Much has been said by modern-day prophets and apostles about the dangers of pride and how it causes us to elevate ourselves. Perhaps this is why Nephi also sees that the pretentious building high in the air has no foundation and that it must fall because it is not supported by eternal realities. It cannot stand because everything and everyone who is not founded on Christ must fall at His coming, "and the fall thereof [will be] exceedingly great" (1 Ne. 11:36; see also Hel. 5:12, Moroni 7:46–47, and D&C 132:14). When Nephi observes how his own seed will also be visited by Christ but will eventually reject Him, forget who they are, and descend into the depths of iniquity, he suddenly understands the mists of darkness (temptations of the devil [see 1 Ne. 12:17]), the river of filthy water (hell [see 1 Ne. 12:16]), and the terrible gulf of justice (see 1 Ne. 12:18) that must separate the wicked from the righteous because they reject their identity and privileges as children of God. Truly, the dream of Lehi is the real story of mortality and beyond. If an angel were showing you the meaning of Lehi's dream as it applies to your life, what would you see?

The Mirages of Mortality

We learn through Lehi's dream that the only way to get to the tree of life and partake of the luscious fruit is by grabbing hold of and clinging to the iron rod—the word of God and the Word of God (see John 1:1-14)—that runs along the narrow path by the fountain of living waters (see 1 Ne. 11:25), the Living Waters of Christ. We learn from Nephi's interpretation that the reason we must cling to the rod of iron and stay strictly on the path is because of those "exceedingly great" (1 Ne. 8:23) mists of darkness—temptations and illusions of the devil (see 1 Ne. 12:17)—that keep us from finding the way to the tree with our own eyes. Some LDS scholars have compared these mists of darkness to the terrifying sandstorms that arise in the Arabian Desert where Lehi and his family were traveling. These storms block out all light and pelt the body relentlessly with countless grains of painful wind-driven sand. How well this symbolizes the unremitting and ruthless fiery darts of Satan! He comes at us from any and every direction, sometimes all at once! He knows that he can rarely trap iron rod people with obvious sin, so he uses physical, emotional, and spiritual weaknesses and imbalances to lead us subtly away if we are not vigilant and diligent. He doesn't care how or why we let go of the iron rod—Christ—he only cares that we weaken our determination or release our grip in some way. To the extent that we lose our grip on Christ we lose our grip on reality and the anchor to our true identity. The great and spacious building then starts looking real and desirable to us. Lehi tells us that even those who are enjoying the fruit of the tree can still be drawn away.

> # Satan doesn't care how or why we let go of the iron rod— he only cares that we lose our grip.

This distraction from the tree of life—away from Jesus Christ, His love, and His Atonement—was brought home to Brent and Wendy in an unforgettable way. One Monday night when their children were still at home, the family studied Lehi's dream in a family home evening lesson. In order to keep the entire family interested, Wendy asked them to read the story and draw a picture of what they thought Lehi (and later Nephi) saw in the dream. Each family member sketched something similar to the layout in the paintings we often see in the *Ensign* magazine, but their youngest daughter added what were clearly Halloween-like eyeballs completely out of their sockets and scattered around on the ground below the tree of life. Puzzled, Wendy asked her what the eyeballs meant. With a straight face, her mischievous daughter replied, "It says, 'after they had partaken of the fruit of the tree they did *cast their eyes about* as if they were ashamed'" (1 Ne. 8:25). She was obviously trying to be funny, but her gimmick actually emphasized a very important part of the story that is an essential key to keeping our grip on the iron rod and our focus on Christ. *Once you have tasted of the incomparable fruit, why even look around when you know that nothing else is real?* Why worry about the scorn of the great and spacious building when you know it is a temporary illusion fabricated by the people who are in it for their own selfish purposes?

Nephi teaches us the plain and simple answer to dealing with the mocking, pointing fingers of the proud—"we heeded them not" (1 Ne. 8:33). If we allow ourselves to be tempted by this temporal distraction that appeals to our carnal pride, we begin to forget the eternal, real, and satisfying fruit we have in our very own hands. To put the warning in today's vernacular, "Don't even think about it!"

Opposition to God

There are countless ways to lose sight of who we are, what we are here for, and what we mean to our Heavenly Father and Savior. Most, if not all of them, have to do with pride—being in opposition to God to one degree or another, refusing to accept the reality that finding and fulfilling our identity means total surrender to and dependence on the Savior and His Atonement. We may make the mistake of thinking we are more than we are and that we don't need the Atonement. We may make the mistake of thinking we are less than we are and that we are not worthy of the Atonement. We may make the mistake of not being content with who we are because we don't appreciate the Atonement and the opportunity just to be here on earth.

While few of us in the Church are tempted to seek after power and fame on a grand scale, we still deal with pride in our own lives, even as we seek daily to humbly live the gospel. Even if pride doesn't lead us to great sin, it still carries what is called an "opportunity cost." What more important and eternally significant blessings are we trading for things of no lasting value? Anytime we give in to pride or selfishness it is because we have traded God for something else.

All of us are especially tempted by the need for approval, acceptance, and attention from those around us. We don't like being left out, made fun of, looked down on, or scorned—all of the very things that come at us from the great and spacious building. This need can wreak havoc in our lives. On the other hand, we may not even do things to please the people in the great and spacious building. We may do things to impress the leaders and members of the Church with our righteousness and good works, as the Pharisees did in Christ's day. But it was still the honors of men they were after—the immediate gratification of their pride. Such pride, taken to the extreme, led them—along with others—to instigate the Crucifixion of the Son of God! "Adulation is poison," President Gordon B. Hinckley was often heard to say. When Christ lived on earth He was never widely accepted. He warned, "Woe unto you, when all men shall speak well of you! for so did their fathers to the false prophets" (Luke 6:26).

Thus, whenever we derive our identity and motivation from the people and things of this world, we are subject to pride. This includes rejecting God and His laws but also encompasses things that some would consider the opposite of pride—self-pity, low self-esteem, letting the world determine self-esteem—all of these are a state of opposition to God and thus to our divine identity. If we find ourselves in these states, we are rejecting our identity just as much as if we are proudly defiant and rebellious. Such states of mind stem from obsession with ourselves and how we don't measure up to others; discontent with what the Lord has allotted us; and unwillingness

> **Belief Window**
> Whose approval do I seek in my actions and appearance each day?

to lose our earthly selves and accept our eternal identity through Christ. Perhaps we could further define pride, then, as rejecting our God-given identity for one of our own making regardless of what motivates it.

We Can't Create Our Own Identity

Many in the world would argue that the only way to find your identity is to be independent, to do things your own way, to refuse to "follow" anyone—especially a prophet of God. They fear they will lose their identity by conforming to the teachings of the gospel. They try to carve out their own neutral territory where they can do as they please but escape the consequences. President Henry B. Eyring pointed out the fallacy of this kind of thinking in mortality. Speaking of Korihor, the anti-Christ who encouraged many to" free" themselves from the constraints of the gospel, he pointed out that Korihor argued that taking counsel from God's servants was in essence surrendering God-given independence. But doing so, says President Eyring, isn't a surrender of independence but the choice of a different influence—it is moving from a Father who wants to give us all He has out of love to a being whose whole purpose is to make us miserable out of his hatred (see "Safety in Counsel," *Ensign*, June 2008, 4–9).

This is our eternal reality, and it simply cannot be changed—nor would we want it to be. Satan was cast out of heaven for trying to convince God's children that eternal truths could be manipulated. Eternal truths

Identity Check

"The proud stand more in fear of men's judgment than of God's judgment. (See D&C 3:6–7; D&C 30:1–2; D&C 60:2.) 'What will men think of me?' weighs heavier than 'What will God think of me?'

"Fear of men's judgment manifests itself in competition for men's approval. The proud love 'the praise of men more than the praise of God.' (John 12:42–43.) Our motives for the things we do are where the sin is manifest. Jesus said He did 'always those things' that pleased God. (John 8:29.) Would we not do well to have the pleasing of God as our motive rather than to try to elevate ourselves above our brother and outdo another?

"When pride has a hold on our hearts, we lose our independence of the world and deliver our freedoms to the bondage of men's judgment. The world shouts louder than the whisperings of the Holy Ghost. The reasoning of men overrides the revelations of God, and the proud let go of the iron rod. (See 1 Ne. 8:19–28; 1 Ne. 11:25; 1 Ne. 15:23–24.)"

—President Ezra Taft Benson, "Beware of Pride," *Ensign*, May 1989, 4

are manifestations of eternal love. Another immutable eternal truth is that even when pride obscures our view of our true identity, there is no question about who we are and how Heavenly Father and His Son feel about us. In *reality*, knowing our eternal identity should be enough to keep us clinging to the iron rod. Admittedly, arriving at that state of contentment with our divine selves is a lifelong process that is only possible through Christ and His Atonement. But for our part, we must be willing to submit and be changed. As long as we seek to do our own will instead of God's will, we still have pride.

Humility—A Reality Check

President Ezra Taft Benson taught that "the antidote for pride is humility—meekness, submissiveness. (See Alma 7:23.) It is the broken heart and contrite spirit. (See 3 Ne. 9:20; 3 Ne. 12:19; D&C 20:37; D&C 59:8; Ps. 34:18; Isa. 57:15; Isa. 66:2.)."

It takes humility and careful daily introspection to examine our true motives for the things we do. If we don't question ourselves under the guidance of the Holy Spirit, we may never recognize the bits and pieces of pride still encrusting our hearts. If we don't continually fine-tune our will to the Lord's will, we may get off the strait and narrow path. Humility is not a personality trait that some have and some don't. As President Benson pointed out, humility is a choice we make:

> We can choose to humble ourselves by loving God, sub-mitting our will to His, and putting Him first in our lives. (See 3 Ne. 11:11; 3 Ne. 13:33; Moro. 10:32.)
>
> We must yield "to the enticings of the Holy Spirit," put off the prideful "natural man," become "a saint through the atonement of Christ the Lord," and become "as a child, submissive, meek, humble." (Mosiah 3:19; see also Alma 13:28.) ("Beware of Pride," *Ensign,* May 1986, 7)

Thus our eternal identity and goal is to become humble, submissive children. We are already children of God. That fact can't be changed. But only when we become children of Christ by submission can He lead us back into His Father's kingdom (see Mosiah 5:7) to reclaim the inheritance God has bequeathed to us. That requires the giving of our very selves to Christ.

Finally, Elder Neal A. Maxwell once asserted, "Humility is not the disavowal of our worth; rather, it is the sober realization of how much we are valued by God" (Cory H. Maxwell, ed., *Neal A. Maxwell Quote Book* [Salt Lake City: Bookcraft, 2001], 165). True humility will result when *you* have received a testimony from Heavenly Father of *your* great worth to Him. It is humbling to know that the God and Creator of all life is your own personal Father. He knows you, answers your prayers, is aware of your life, cares about every aspect of your life, and loves you perfectly. When you realize that Heavenly Father allowed His Only Begotten Son, Jesus Christ, to die for you personally, it is even more humbling.

Humility is realizing how very precious we are to Heavenly Father and the Savior. Humility is also the key to understanding our true identity because when we are humble, we know that without Christ we have no life, no future. But because of His Atonement, Christ promises that we will be blessed with all that He has. Our individuality and identity will blossom and grow to its infinite capacity through His power to set us free.

Why Is My Body So Important to My Earthly and Eternal Identity?

THE BODY IS PART OF the soul and therefore is essential to our identity both here and hereafter (see D&C 88:15). Yet, very few if any worldly philosophies or religions today teach that the soul is both body and spirit. Furthermore, few religions teach the reality of the Resurrection—a reuniting of the spirit and the body after they have been temporarily separated by death. Many view the resurrection as simply the continuation of the spirit through eternity; to some, that includes the loss of individuality through union with God.

This idea may partly stem from the false idea that God does not have a body. This mistaken doctrine has perhaps contributed more to the theft of our knowledge of our eternal identity than any other false doctrine in the history of mankind. Once this truth was lost, it is easier to see why many other important doctrines relating to our true identity were abandoned or obscured. Many no longer believed man to be literally created in God's physical image. This made it easier to dismiss the idea that we are actual children of God. Our spirits no longer needed a premortal existence or a bodily resurrection—and, worst of all, mankind could never even think of becoming like God. Such beliefs became heresy. Bodies were often viewed as a

> The false idea that God does not have a body has perhaps contributed more to the theft of our eternal identity than any other false doctrine in the history of mankind.

punishment, treated as the enemy to be hated or as disposable vehicles of hedonistic pleasure and indulgence. With the scientific advocacy of the origin and evolution of man from animals, many in our day have happily concluded that there is no God to whom they are accountable—their body is their own, and they can do with it as they please. Others have sorrowfully accepted the fact that life is merely survival of the fittest and that mortal life is their only reality. They have no hope in Christ for a better world and a glorious resurrection. It is easy to see the influence of the adversary in false doctrines that denigrate or deny the eternal reality of the body.

With the Restoration of the gospel, the Prophet Joseph Smith clarified how essential a true understanding of the nature of God the Father and the resurrected Christ are to our understanding of our identity. He declared boldly, "If men do not comprehend the character of God, they do not comprehend themselves" (*Teachings of the Prophet Joseph Smith*, Joseph Fielding Smith, comp. [Salt Lake City: Deseret Book, 1976], 294). Surely the "character of God" includes His physical nature as well. We are clearly taught in D&C 130:22 that our Heavenly Father does indeed have a glorified, resurrected body of flesh and bones, as does the Lord Jesus Christ. We are made in the literal image of our Heavenly Father spiritually *and* physically. We also learn from modern revelation that there is no such thing as immaterial matter. All spirit is matter, and spirit matter is more refined than temporal matter (see D&C 131:7–8). The Prophet Joseph Smith further taught that we came to earth to gain a body "and present it pure before God in the celestial kingdom. *The great principle of happiness consists in having a body*" (*Teachings of the Prophet Joseph Smith*, Joseph Fielding Smith, comp. [Salt Lake City: Deseret Book, 1976], 181; emphasis added).

Your soul—both your body and your spirit—is your true identity here in mortality and will be forever when you are resurrected. After death, spirits who are temporarily separated from their bodies in the spirit world feel incomplete and limited without their bodies; they look upon the time of this separation as bondage and wait anxiously for Christ to deliver them from it (see D&C 45:17; 138:15, 50). Joseph Smith learned that "the elements are eternal, and spirit and element, inseparably connected, receive a fullness of joy; and when separated, man cannot receive a fullness of joy" (D&C 93:33, 34). Only when reunited with their bodies, never again to be separated, can spirits progress toward ultimate godhood and happiness.

Furthermore, "the spirit and the body shall be reunited again in its perfect form; both limb and joint shall be restored to its proper frame, even as we now are at this time" (Alma 11:43). The universal Resurrection that comes to all of us as an unconditional gift of Christ corrects any malady or disability we may have had in mortality. Resurrection ensures that every part of our body will be restored to its proper functioning and perfect frame (see Alma 11:45). We will not receive a different body at the time of the resurrection. Resurrection, as the Book of Mormon teaches, is a perfect restoration—not a replacement or re-creation—of the very body we have now, but quickened and infused with eternal glory and immortality. That glorified, resurrected body—inseparably connected with our immortal, divine spirit—will be our identity forever. Because of that, the body should be viewed just as reverently as the spirit.

Understanding these doctrines concerning souls, spirits, and bodies makes all the difference in how we as Latter-day Saints should view our mortal tabernacles. Without continually reminding ourselves of these remarkable truths, we may forget that our bodies are a sacred temple for our spirits and for the Spirit of God that dwells in us, sanctifies us, and guides us back to Him. We may forget that they are a miraculous gift and a tangible token of God's love—a reward for our premortal faithfulness. In our frustrations with the challenges of mortality, we may

Without these remarkable truths, we may forget that our bodies are a sacred temple for our spirits and for the Spirit of God that dwells in us.

not remember that they are contributing to our learning and progression.

Because we often lose sight of these truths, we may not care for our bodies as we would a holy temple; we may not regard them as the body of a prince or princess, a future god or goddess. We may feel that we must merely tolerate our body until one day we get it back resurrected and perfected. Yet your body is the only material thing you will take with you from your time on earth. The way you treat and feel about your body helps shape not only how you feel about yourself here on earth, but potentially the extent to which you recognize and appreciate your eternal identity. Just as the "man is not without the woman, neither the woman without the man" (see 1 Cor. 11:11), neither is the spirit without the body nor the body without the spirit in the great plan of salvation.

Perhaps it also helps to think of the relationship between spirit and body by seeing the spirit as being symbolic of faith while the body may be symbolic of works. We know that faith without works is dead (see James 2:20), but works without faith likewise have no eternal life or meaning. The argument over faith and works has raged for centuries. Which is more important? C. S. Lewis insightfully compares faith and works to the two blades of a pair of scissors: Both are equally important. Both are equally indispensible because the scissors are useless without either blade (see *Mere Christianity* [New York: Harper Collins, 1980], 129). For some reason that we do not yet fully understand, the body is just as essential for exaltation as is the spirit.

The temple also teaches the sacredness of the body. Not only are the temple ordinances, like the body, required for exaltation, but it is required that those ordinances be administered *to* the mortal body. That is why we must serve as proxy for the dead in work they can no longer do without their mortal tabernacles. Like a temple being dedicated to the Lord, the body, along with the spirit, is there endowed with powerful blessings intended to prosper, protect, and prepare us for this life and eternity. We are given special sacred clothing to cover and protect the body and help keep it holy. Also in the temple we consecrate all that we have been given, including our bodies, to the Lord.

Since our bodies came from God, were ransomed from death and sin by the Savior, and will be resurrected through Him, they really don't belong to us anyway. The Apostle Paul reminded the Saints of his day, "What? know ye not that your body is the temple of the Holy Ghost which is in you, which ye have of God, and ye are not your own? For ye are bought with a price: therefore glorify God in your body and your spirit, which are God's" (1 Cor. 6:19–20). And what is the price that was paid so that we may one day have these bodies and spirits united, sanctified, and glorified forever? "Forasmuch as ye know that ye were not redeemed with corruptible things, as silver and gold . . . But with the precious blood of Christ, as of a lamb without blemish and without spot" (1 Pet. 1:18). In a measure, our love and gratitude for the Savior, who paid the ultimate and infinite price to ransom our souls is reflected in how we view and treat both body and spirit. What we do to our body is often symbolic of what we are doing to our spirits.

Working Relationship between the Body and Spirit Here on Earth

On earth our bodies and spirits lead us to a measure, though not a fullness, of happiness. The body and spirit are designed as a single, sacred, whole being even while on earth. As previously mentioned, some have the misconception that the body and spirit are antagonists that are not designed to be compatible. Therefore, some have concluded that the spirit gets stronger by stifling the body. Perhaps it would be better to say that the spirit gets stronger by training the body, and the body becomes stronger by helping to shape and provide a foundation or expression for the spirit.

As Latter-day Saints we may also sometimes erroneously believe that the doctrine of "putting off the natural man" (see Mosiah 3:19) means that our bodies are somehow an enemy to be shunned or suppressed. Some believe the term *natural man* refers only to the body. But we know that spiritually we are also cut off from the presence of God because of the Fall of Adam and Eve (see Alma 42:7). We know that without the Atonement of Christ, our spirits would become angels to the devil (see 2 Ne. 9:9), but we do not share the belief of other religions in the total depravity of man. Many believe that man—both body and spirit—is inherently evil. Even though we, by reason of the Fall, are cut off from the immediate presence of God, we all have a vital element of the divine within us. Our spirits are of divine origin. As daughters and sons of God we possess a divine DNA, so to speak, and

---

Identity Check

"When you are tempted, buffeted, and step out of the way inadvertently; when you are overtaken in a fault, or commit an overt act unthinkingly; when you are full of evil passion, and wish to yield to it, then stop and let the spirit, which God has put in your tabernacles, take the lead. If you do that, I will promise you that you will overcome all evil, and obtain eternal lives. But many, very many let the spirit yield to the body, and are overcome and destroyed.

"But let your body rise up with its passions, with fallen nature pertaining to it, and let the spirit yield to it, your destruction is sure. On the other hand, let the spirit take the lead, and bring the body and its passions into subjection, and you are safe."

—President Brigham Young, *Journal of Discourses*, 2:256

our spirit beings are filled with intelligence—God's light and truth and power, that the scriptures call the Light of Christ, which is in and through all things (see D&C 88:7–13; 93:29–30). We also bring to earth foreordinations, personal tendencies for righteousness, and desires and longings for heaven acquired in the premortal existence. These are even stronger among those who were faithful and righteous there. Thus, we live in a fallen world where the natural man is an enemy to God (Mosiah 3:19) but still has the potential to be divine—created, both body and spirit, in the image of God.

The Spirit Directs the Body

When we speak of physical or bodily appetites, we may mistakenly convey the notion that the body is in charge of our actions. The scriptures teach us that spirit acts and that element is acted upon. Element does not have agency or the capacity to act for itself, but element, by nature, is acted upon. The body is element and is the instrument of our mind and spirit. The body, with its natural tendencies and cravings, may send signals to the brain, but in reality, the spirit controls the body's actions. When our spirit—the real control center of the soul—is weak, we may choose to act upon "natural man" impulses and do things that adversely affect both body and spirit.

On the other hand, when our spirit is strong and healthy—"fed" and "conditioned" by the Holy Spirit—our bodies respond accordingly.

In reality, it takes a lifetime of practice to bring the body in subjection to the spirit, something that can be effectively done only through faith in the Lord Jesus Christ. King Benjamin explained the process as becoming "a saint through the atonement of Christ the Lord" (Mosiah 3:19). Elder Jeffrey R. Holland insightfully observed that while all of us have divine potential, we are in a fallen state, and some elements of our nature require restraint and discipline. It is as though we are made of raw

> It takes a lifetime of practice to bring the body in subjection to the spirit, something that can be done only through the Lord Jesus Christ.

ingredients that need to be harnessed and focused so they, and we, can achieve our divine potential. How grateful we should be, pointed out Elder Holland, that our Heavenly Father's influence can help us turn those elements into a blessing instead of a curse (see *Christ and the New Covenant* [Salt Lake City: Deseret Book, 2006], 207).

To a great extent, then, our bodies are affected by the choices of our spirits and how fully we rely on and exercise faith in the Atonement of Christ. Have you ever noticed that over time a person's life choices are so often visible in his or her body and countenance?

The Body Helps Influence the Spirit

We can further appreciate what a wonderful benefit our bodies are to our spirits here in mortality. What greater way to demonstrate our desire to follow Christ and become like Him in every way than to come to earth and gain a body that we may teach, discipline, and train up to one day present pure before Him? Consider the old Greek myth about Sisyphus, the king who was punished by the gods by being condemned to an eternity of rolling a huge bolder up a hill only to watch it roll down again. We may sometimes feel like trying to discipline our bodies is a Sisyphean feat, with little or no progress and no end in sight. But this myth doesn't take into account the great spiritual muscle that can be developed in the long-term repetition of back-breaking and soul-stretching labor. It may be that the spirit is taught and trained more thoroughly when it has the body as a foundation or extension, similar to what happens when we add weights or resistance to physical exercise. Perhaps the individual weaknesses or strengths, handicaps or abilities, beauty or homeliness given to us in our bodies are the molds that will help shape the unique spiritual growth each of us needs to fulfill our mission on earth and succeed in being prepared for eternal life.

Elder David A. Bednar reminded that the many things we experience in mortality—including things like happiness, sorrow, joy, pain, and even physical limitations—are the things that prepare us for eternity. The scriptures teach us that many of our lessons and experiences must be learned "according to the flesh" (1 Ne. 19:6) (see "Things As They Really Are," *Brigham Young University 2009–2010 Devotional and Fireside Speeches*, May 2009, 2). Keeping Elder Bednar's observation in mind, we must also consider that altering or misusing our bodies for our own selfish purposes may alter and even destroy some of God's purposes for them.

The Body Is an Advantage

Perhaps most important, prophets have taught that the body gives us at least some advantage over Satan in this life. So while it might sometimes seem that life would be easier without a body, exactly the opposite is true. The adversary and those who followed him will never be given the gift of a body "and herein is [their] punishment," taught the Prophet Joseph Smith, and "all beings who have bodies have power over those who have not" (*Teachings of the Prophet Joseph Smith,* Joseph Fielding Smith, comp. [Salt Lake City: Deseret Book, 1976], 181).

For whatever reasons we need these bodies of ours here on earth, thankfully none of those reasons depends on having perfect or beautiful bodies right now. At the same time, we know that they will be perfected and beautified in the next life through the Atonement of Christ if we use them well in this life. President Lorenzo Snow confirmed, "We will have our bodies glorified, made free from every sickness and distress, and rendered most beautiful. There is nothing more beautiful to look upon than a resurrected man or woman" (*Teachings of Lorenzo Snow: Fifth President of the Church of Jesus Christ of Latter-day Saints* [Salt Lake City: Bookcraft, 1996], 99). So let's rejoice and be grateful that we have a body, regardless of its present beauty. It means we are on our way to exaltation!

> Let's rejoice and be grateful that we have a body, regardless of its present beauty. It means we are on our way to exaltation!

Satan's Insidious Assaults on the Body

Satan hates us because we have a body, and much of his effort is obviously directed at getting us to misuse and abuse it. That fact should sober us with the realization of the body's importance to our eternal identity and progression. Satan despises the fact that we are embodied and will be resurrected. The body is so important in Heavenly Father's plan of happiness, says Elder Bednar, that Satan wants to frustrate that plan both by persuading us to minimize the importance of the body and by tempting us to misuse it—things against which we need to be on constant guard (see Bednar, 2–3).

Let's look at just a few of the countless insidious ways through which Satan tempts us to misuse and minimize our physical bodies in today's society.

"Not Good Enough"

Have you ever given someone a gift that you took great pains to select, pay for, wrap, and deliver only to see it soon afterward neglected, destroyed, or thoughtlessly discarded somewhere? Surely it is painful to our Heavenly Father (who created these bodies) and to our Savior (who ransomed them with His excruciating sacrifice) to see them go unappreciated—or, worse, hated.

Our bodies are living things. The Light of Christ is in and through them (see D&C 88:13, 41). Why, then, do we often have such negative and critical feelings about them just because they don't meet Satanically inspired standards of perfection and beauty? That is not their purpose. They are doing their job! Hardly anyone improves under constant criticism but almost everyone improves under love and acceptance. Our bodies were intended to be loved, nurtured, appreciated, covered, protected, and disciplined.

As with a spouse or child, we must stop finding fault with our bodies, forget about our need for mortal approval, and derive our self-esteem from how much the Lord loves them—not how they look to the rest of the world. Taking care of our body starts with recognizing it as the miraculous gift it is, being grateful to the Lord for it, and showing that gratitude by loving and nurturing it.

Dishonoring Our Bodies through Sin

Some forms of misusing our bodies are obviously among the worst sins we can commit. This type of misuse brings to mind the Apostle Paul's reference to those who were given "up to uncleanness through the lusts of their own hearts, to dishonour their own bodies between themselves" (Rom. 1: 24). In our day, this would include all forms of immorality—all mental, emotional, and physical sexual relations outside of the sacred marriage covenant relationship, including pornography and other addictive sexually oriented misbehaviors. Perhaps the only thing worse than dishonoring our own body is to dishonor someone else's body. Just because we are only looking at an image doesn't mean we aren't degrading ourselves, others, and God's sacred procreation process.

What sorrow it must bring to our Heavenly Father and our Savior to see what is done on earth with the miraculous bodies They have freely provided for each of us! In fact, we get a sobering and deeply moving glimpse of the pain They feel at the lack of respect that Their children have for each other in the book of Moses. Though this passage certainly encompasses all kinds of evil, sins of body abuse are certainly at the forefront. When Enoch is speaking face-to-face with the Lord, the Lord weeps as He and Enoch gaze upon the inhabitants of the earth:

> And Enoch said unto the Lord: How is it that thou canst weep, seeing thou art holy, and from all eternity to all eternity? . . .
>
> The Lord said unto Enoch: Behold these thy brethren; they are the *workmanship of mine own hands*, and I gave unto them their knowledge, in the day I created them; and in the Garden of Eden, gave I unto man his agency;
>
> And unto thy brethren have I said, and also given commandment, that they should love one another, and that they should choose me, their Father; but behold, they are without affection, and they *hate their own blood* [bodies]. (Moses 7:29, 32–33; emphasis added)

Realizing who we really are and that our bodies are a sacred, dearly purchased gift should help us treat them and the bodies of others in reverent and respectful ways. We will be held accountable for how we treat both. Fortunately, because of the Atonement of Christ, it is not too late to make changes if necessary in the way we treat and view our body and the bodies of others.

Substance Abuse and Other Addictive Behaviors

We are all thankfully familiar with the health laws revealed by the Lord. The Word of Wisdom (see D&C 89) is a miraculous, protective revelation given long before science and society had any idea how widespread and devastating the abuse of alcohol, tobacco, and other addictive substances would be physically, emotionally, and spiritually. The consequences of such things should be more than obvious today and we ought to thank the Lord every day for the protection afforded us by knowledge of and obedience to the Word of Wisdom.

While the Word of Wisdom does not specifically mention today's mind-altering drugs, prophets have certainly indicated that such substances are also implied by the spirit of that revelation. Even so, drug abuse of all kinds, especially prescription drug abuse, is reaching its strangling fingers deeper and deeper into the membership of the Church. While we don't want to make judgments about why people start using drugs, we must be more protective and vigilant concerning our bodies in this day and age, just as we would be with our children. Satan has discovered a great opportunity here to enslave otherwise faithful but unsuspecting Church members. From now on, we must proceed with great caution. This is a time when we need the direction and protection of the Holy Spirit perhaps more than at any other time in the history of the world.

Indeed, each of us is admonished to seek for personal revelation. Living according to the promptings of the Holy Ghost is one of the great purposes of mortality. When the body and spirit are in tune with each other and in tune with the Holy Ghost, the channels are open for personal revelation. Moreover, while our bodies need physical food and our spirits need spiritual food, the body usually functions better (obeys the spirit) when the spirit is nourished and the spirit functions better when the body is strong and the mind is clear. If we are casual in our adherence to the Word of Wisdom, we may inadvertently diminish the effectiveness of our bodies in the crucial process of receiving personal revelation. If we are deeply respectful of our bodies and strive to understand the profound promises of living the Word of Wisdom, we may experience personal revelation and blessings from the Holy Ghost beyond anything we have yet experienced.

> When the body and spirit are in tune with each other and in tune with the Holy Ghost, the channels are open for personal revelation.

This begs the question we must each ask ourselves: *What am I missing out on because I am not taking care of my body?* We are promised that "All Saints who remember to keep and do these sayings . . . shall receive health in their navel and marrow to their bones . . . and shall run and not be weary, and shall walk and not faint" (D&C 89:18–20). Do we live up to our privileges in this regard? The *For the Strength of Youth* pamphlet reminds us that "the Lord has commanded you to take good care of your body. To do this, observe the Word of Wisdom, found in Doctrine and Covenants 89. Eat nutritious food, exercise regularly, and get enough sleep. When you do all these things, you remain free from harmful addictions and have control over your life. You gain the blessings of a healthy body, an alert mind, and the guidance of the Holy Ghost. Never let Satan or others lead you to think that breaking the Word of Wisdom will make you happier or more attractive" (36–37).

> As we receive temple ordinances, our bodies become formally dedicated to their higher destinies, and we begin to gain access to great hidden treasures of knowledge.

Finally, we must live by the basic precepts of the Word of Wisdom to be considered worthy to enter the holy temple and have our bodies anointed and endowed with great blessings of strength, protection, and consecration. As we receive temple ordinances, our bodies become formally dedicated to their higher destinies and we begin to gain access to the great "hidden treasures" (D&C 89:19) of knowledge we are promised for honoring our bodies.

Minimizing Our Bodies

In a CES Fireside given in 2009, Elder David A. Bednar expressed a serious concern about a growing modern problem, one that probably never existed before the advent of high-tech media or any of the other unprecedented forms of private personal communication. He issued a strong warning that the misuse of video gaming and various types of electronic communication may be minimizing the importance of our bodies. He issued a powerful warning that the adversary delights in causing people to disconnect from things as they really are and to instead become so fixated on all the digital means of communication that they give up the reward of person-to-person communication. When we fall victim to that temptation and become addicted to the Internet and other types of digital media, we become almost as we were in a premortal, unembodied state, and we surrender the full experience of having a body (see "Things As They Really Are," *Brigham Young University 2009–2010 Devotional and Fireside Speeches*, May 2009, 5).

This prophetic counsel is so needed today. People of all ages are often innocently engaging in computer-directed relationships that basically ignore or even deliberately alter their true identity. Virtual reality is replacing true reality. The result is a form of identity theft that may seem innocuous at first but could result in tragic consequences. If our experiences in the body are so crucial to our progress, what happens when we minimize those opportunities? Elder Bednar posed some insightful questions to protect us. We need to ask ourselves whether our use of the media and various technologies impedes or invites the constant companionship of the Holy Ghost and whether the time we spend on technology and media impacts our ability to love and serve others (see "Things As They Really Are," *Brigham Young University 2009–2010 Devotional and Fireside Speeches*, May 2009, 9).

All of us know of or have heard of instances in which people have become trapped in the alluring and deceptive world of virtual reality. They give their souls to something that does not really exist but that can have very real consequences in real life. They may become numbed to the world around them, dead inside, or even addicted. Some are even seduced into real-life sins or physical harm. Satan is tech-savvy and sin-savvy, and even when

> Virtual reality is replacing true reality. The result is a form of identity theft that could result in tragic consequences.

he can't get us to use media to view or participate in evil, he can often get us to go overboard and lose our sense of what is most important in life. He may ultimately cut us off from developing true charity—the pure love of Christ—for ourselves, others, and the Lord Himself. The Apostle Paul warns us that without charity, we are nothing (see 1 Cor. 13:2). In other words, we forfeit the fulfillment of our identity as followers of Christ.

Finally, balance, wisdom, and self-respect personify a healthy approach to life. The physical activities in which we engage also say a lot about how much we appreciate our bodies and the precious gift of life that is in them. Going to extremes may be another way of not respecting our bodies. Elder Bednar spoke to this when he counseled that going to unusual and dangerous extremes not only jeopardizes our physical well-being, puts at risk the body with which God intends that we receive the learning experiences of mortality, and in a very real way diminishes that body (see "Things As They Really Are," *Brigham Young University 2009–2010 Devotional and Fireside Speeches*, May 2009, 4). Is it any wonder that we have been advised to observe moderation in *all* things?

We Get to Choose

Even though our body is not our own, God will rarely intervene if we choose to treat it badly. Neither will He intervene in the consequences of our choices unless we repent and submit to His will for our bodies. Having a body in this life is not about bringing it to perfection. It is about bringing it, along with our spirit, into submission—submission to Christ by yielding to the promptings of the Holy Ghost. This happens most readily when there is harmony of body and spirit.

> The physical activities in which we engage say a lot about how much we appreciate our bodies and the precious gift of life that is in them.

We do not have to undergo any major expense or take extreme actions to be at peace with our bodies. Knowing our identity and nature and being grateful for them is the beginning of this complementary relationship between body and soul. When we are tempted with negative thoughts about our bodies and ourselves, we can remember our true identity and the true purposes of our bodies. We can express our thankfulness to Heavenly Father that He has given us a body and allowed us to progress one major step closer to becoming like Him. When we genuinely feel this gratitude, we will be less apt to be critical of our body or think ill of what we have been given.

Regardless of the exact nature of our body, we can be grateful for who we are, trusting in the resurrection and our eventual wholeness through the blessed Atonement of our Savior. When we give up a self-absorbed obsession with our bodies and focus on Christ, we begin to see our bodies in their true light. Indeed, "if your eye be single to my glory, your *whole bodies* shall be filled with light, and there shall be no darkness in you; and that body which is filled with light comprehendeth all things" (D&C 88:67; emphasis added)—especially its true identity and eternal potential.

WHY IS UNDERSTANDING GOD'S LOVE SO ESSENTIAL TO UNDERSTANDING MY IDENTITY?

THE LOVE OF HEAVENLY FATHER and Jesus Christ is more than just a powerful feeling of affection and concern; Their love is expressed explicitly in our identity and in the Atonement and the plan of salvation that were instituted on our behalf. One perfectly equals the other. Their perfect love made the plan and the Atonement not only possible but inevitable.

Furthermore, love originates with the Godhead. "We love Him, because He first loved us" (1 John 4:19). The scriptures teach us that God is love and that God never changes (see 1 John 4; Mormon 9:9). God's love is constant. President Gordon B. Hinckley likened God's love to the Polar or North Star because it is always there for us. Elder Jeffrey R. Holland has assured us that the first commandment—to love God with all our heart, might, mind, and strength—was given to us on earth because the first promise in heaven must be that God will always love us with those same qualities (or in that same manner) (see "Look to God and Live," *Ensign*, Nov. 1993, 14).

The Atonement is the greatest gift of love we will ever receive. Though universal, it is a highly personal gift that is granted to each person as if he or she were the only one for whom Christ died. Clearly this is not something that we could ever earn but is freely given. Yet, until we accept and experience Christ's love for us and for others, we cannot be fully "at-one" with Him. We cannot fully appreciate our identity.

Our identity remains vulnerable to those who

The Atonement is the greatest gift of love we will ever receive.

would rob us of our understanding of it. Once we have truly tasted His love, however, we catch a vision of the truth of who we really are (see

Mosiah 4:11–16). And as Elder D. Todd Christofferson testified, once you feel even the very smallest part of Christ's love for you, the resulting personal security will stimulate an increase in your love for Him and for your Heavenly Father (see "When Thou Art Converted," *Ensign*, May 2004, 12). Their love is so powerful that simply tasting of it bears witness of your worth and changes the way you see yourself.

The early Christian Apostles used the Greek word *agape* to express this unparalleled kind of love that can come only from God. *Agape* is a love that is pure, perfect, and eternal. It is mercifully extended to each person simply because of the nature of the giver. It is the source of all true love; it is a love so great that no mortal can extend it to another without divine aid. English scriptures translate it as "charity." Elder Jeffrey R. Holland once wrote that God the Father and the Savior Jesus Christ can't help but love us because it is in Their very nature (see "Come Unto Me," *Ensign*, April 1998, 19.) Truly, God is love! That is His nature! There is no doubt that our Heavenly Father loves each and every one of His children. There are no exceptions!

The plan of salvation, especially the Atonement, is the epitome and the natural outcome of the love of the Father and the Son. "For God so loved the world that He gave His only begotten Son" (John 3:16) "For He doeth not anything save it be for the benefit of the world, for He loveth the world, even that he layeth down his own life that he may draw all men unto him" (2 Ne. 26:24). Further ample evidence of God's love is obvious all around us if we open ourselves to receive it, as the lyrics to one of our favorite hymns illustrate:

> Earth, with her ten thousand flow'rs,
> Air, with all its beams and show'rs,
> Heaven's infinite expanse,
> Sea's resplendent countenance—
> All around and all above
> Bear this record: God is love.
>
> Sounds among the vales and hills,
> In the woods and by the rills,
> Of the breeze and of the bird,
> By the gentle murmur stirred—
> Sacred songs, beneath, above,
> Have one chorus: God is love.

All the hopes that sweetly start
From the fountain of the heart,
All the bliss that ever comes
To our earthly human homes,
All the voices from above
Sweetly whisper: God is love.
(Thomas R. Taylor, "God Is Love," *Hymns*, no. 87)

The testimonies of God's love around us are countless. They also include special, individualized messages and blessings to each of us that say, in essence, "I know you. I am aware of your every thought and need. I love you. Come to me, trust in me, and let me make you whole. Let me give you all that I have and all that I am." Each of us can attest to such messages if we are open to recognizing and receiving them.

Yet, so often we ask the wrong questions regarding Heavenly Father's love for us. There are times we might ask ourselves, "Does God really love *me*?" For instance, if we have done something wrong, we may erroneously assume God can't love us because we are "bad." The problem with these kinds of questions is that they are focusing on *us*. The crucial component regarding God's love is not us but God. When we are feeling unlovable, the real question we must ask ourselves is, are we receiving God's love? God's love is a gift, freely given to each of us. It is up to us to receive that gift. In the scriptures we are asked, "For what doth it profit a man if a gift is bestowed upon him, and he receive not the gift? Behold, he rejoices not in that which is given unto him, neither rejoices in him who is the giver of the gift" (D&C 88:33). If we do not receive God's gift of love, then we do not rejoice in or enjoy our own identity or the marvelous blessings that come with His love and His Atonement. And as this scripture testifies, we not only miss the benefits of His love but we also miss out on coming to personally know God, our

> So often we ask the wrong questions about Heavenly Father's love for us. The crucial component in God's love for us is not us, but God.

Father. As we mentioned, God's love is very personal, very individual. When we do receive His love, we also receive Him into our lives in a very personal way. Heavenly Father becomes a very significant reality in our lives day to day. And to know God is to come to know ourselves.

This is certainly not easy. There are many challenges and obstacles to receiving God's love. The main reason for this is that the adversary does not want us to be filled with God's great love. If our hearts are filled with Heavenly Father's love, it will be impossible for the devil to make us miserable "like unto himself" (2 Ne. 9:9). Receiving God's love is a great way to put Satan behind us (see Mark 8:33), to minimize his influence.

Let's explore some of the more common obstacles to receiving God's love. Most of them boil down to fear, and fear usually boils down to pride—an unhealthy and unholy dependence on self.

Belief Window

Am I open to receiving the Lord's love for me?

Do I question His ability to love me?

Fear of Being Unloved

In 1 John 4:18 we read, "There is no fear in love; but perfect love casteth out fear: because fear hath torment. He that feareth is not made perfect in love." God's love is the only source of perfect love and the only true antidote for fear. Just as faith and fear are opposites, so love and fear are also opposites. Fear keeps us from trusting God—His power, His attributes, and His purposes for us. We cannot feel God's love without having faith in Him, and we cannot exercise true faith in Him without feeling His love in return.

A wonderful definition of faith found in *Preach My Gospel* shows how faith in God and trust in His love go hand in hand: "Faith in Him means that you trust Him and are confident that He loves you" ([Salt Lake City: The Church of Jesus Christ of Latter-day Saints, 2004, 116). Usually when we feel fear it is an indication that we need to turn to Heavenly Father and do all we can to more fully receive His love. This is difficult because it requires faith in Heavenly Father and Jesus Christ to overcome the fear that is tending to rob us of our faith. But even faith in God the size of a tiny mustard seed will help set us on the right path. Without confidence that He loves us, we cannot fully exercise faith that He has our best interests at heart—so without faith we cannot understand who we really are.

The love of God can also help us form human relationships out of confidence and healthy self-respect rather than out of fear. Too often a desperate need for human love and approval comes from a fear of being unloved. We may have a fear that we are of little significance or importance. We may feel that we are not worthy of love and therefore deserve whatever treatment we get. Not having respect for ourselves keeps us from expecting others to treat us with respect. The same low self-esteem and self-loathing can also have the opposite effect. We may treat others the same negative way we treat ourselves. Or when we don't trust in God we may have the feeling of needing to be in control of our own lives and everything that happens to us. Sometimes this extends to a need to control others—unrighteous dominion. Controlling behavior is a major obstacle to receiving God's love. The irony is that receiving and trusting in God's love may be the only way to cease from feeling the need to control others or be controlled by them. Elder James E. Faust was often heard to counsel others, "Never take counsel from your fears." On the other hand, we can always take counsel from love, the pure love of God.

It feels so good to have someone love us; it is one of the greatest joys of life. But this should come in addition to the basic love from God that fills our being. But love from others is the frosting on the cake, so to speak. Even when we lose human love we can still stand strong, fulfilled, and confident in God's love. Love from God enables us to stand independent. Yet, it is a natural thing that we be constantly dependent only on His love and goodness because He is the eternal, divine source of our reality, our being.

> **Belief Window**
>
> Do I believe God still loves me even when I make mistakes?
>
> Am I afraid he won't love me if I am not always "good enough"?

Believing We Must Earn God's Love

It is so easy to get caught up in an "earning" mentality. When we lose sight of our God-given reality, we tend to take a false sense of identity from the world around us. In that context, with all the pressures to be somebody, we may fall into the trap of thinking that we are compelled to create our own identity. In creating this false sense of identity, we tend to think that we have to do something to earn the love and approval of others, do something to measure up. This kind of thinking could be part of many aspects of our life—our appearance; the development and performance of talents such as music, sports, dance, or theater; how well we do in school or in our work; how much money we have; where we live; whether or not we marry and whom we marry; how many children we have, how well our children are doing in society, and how well they're doing in the Church; or the level of education we have attained. The list is endless.

> When we lose sight of our God-given reality, we tend to take a false sense of identity from the world around us.

As previously discussed, the impact of this pressure is enormous. The false perception is that if we meet these high worldly standards we are lovable. If we do not, we are not acceptable to ourselves or to others. Apply this kind of thinking to any of these areas, and we are basically describing the stressful way in which most people live—a condition that leads to all kinds of negative behaviors, such as thinking we can never do enough, we can never be enough, we are not loved, we can never be loved, and we are not appreciated for what we do. It also may cause us to compete with others and resent their successes or goodness. It creates a form of pride.

In this way of thinking we are always thirsty—thirsting after the approval of others, comparing ourselves to others, and almost always feeling like we are coming up short. Behaviors may become obsessive in nature to fill the void. It is not that any of the things we are seeking are bad things in and of themselves. The problem is our motivation. The minute we put something other than God first, we are in trouble, because there is no other valid source of truth, reality, or identity. The scriptures warn us repeatedly to have no other "gods" ahead of Him.

"Worshipping" a false god by putting anything ahead of God ultimately leads us to a dead end—a dead end both spiritually and emotionally. No matter the effort, we retain the void, and the emptiness within ourselves never gets permanently filled. When we understand the reality of God's love, the promises that we will never hunger or thirst and that we will be filled through Him make much more sense. He is helping us to realize that the power of His love gives us a positive sense of self and justifiable self-esteem, which are accompanied by peace and strong feelings of being personally secure. When we are filled with His love, nothing is a real threat to us because nothing else is a source of our worth. Our value or importance as a human being is never in question.

Confusing Worth and Worthiness

Doctrinally, it greatly helps to understand the difference between *worth* and *worthiness*. Like agency and identity, *worth* is divine. Each is a God-given, divinely inherited gift. He has given us the capacity to stand independent, to choose, though we do not have the ability to choose the consequences of our choices. We also cannot change the Atonement: "It is finished," as Christ said (John 19:30). The Atonement is infinite and eternal. It covers all sins and all conditions that come to us by reason of the Fall of Adam and through our own transgressions. From the greatest sinner to the innocent baby—all who have ever lived—all must undergo the transformation that can be wrought upon us only by the saving and sanctifying power of the Atonement in order to progress through the plan of salvation. These are powerful realities that can change our lives if we recognize them and embrace them.

The following separate circles or spheres could represent how our worth and worthiness are never connected and never overlap or intersect. They could also represent what Christ and the Father have already done for us that we can never change and the things we can affect through our own choices.

Amazing strength comes as we perceive ourselves as depicted in these circles. In our individual lives, it plays out like this: "My worth is divine, not in my hands. That means my value, importance, and significance is never in question—never! My very basic human need to be significant is always satisfied. No circumstance of life, no other person can ever reduce my significance or worth. On the

Like agency and identity, worth is divine. Each is a God-given, divinely inherited gift. Our *worth* and *worthiness* are distinct entities.

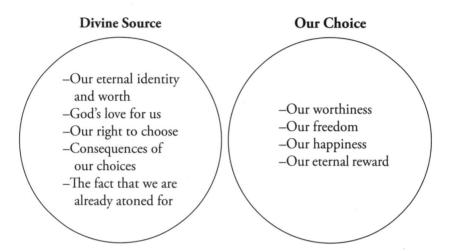

Divine Source

Our Choice

–Our eternal identity
and worth
–God's love for us
–Our right to choose
–Consequences of
our choices
–The fact that we are
already atoned for

–Our worthiness
–Our freedom
–Our happiness
–Our eternal reward

other hand, *my* worthiness is in *my* hands. This is where agency comes in to play. My choices dictate my worthiness. God will help me. I am not left alone to strive to be worthy, but I do need to make correct choices. These choices are apparent in my behavior, my attitudes, and my beliefs. Yet my choices never determine my worth to God. He has already declared that the worth of souls—including mine and yours—is great in his sight" (see D&C 18:15–16).

By keeping worth and worthiness distinct in our minds and hearts, we can derive greater strength. In other words, the two circles should never overlap. If they do, then we have lost perspective concerning our divine nature and our intrinsic worth to our Father in Heaven. We all fall prey at times to thinking that we alone determine our worth. This is a form of the relativism so prevalent today that basically takes God out of the picture. We are saying that everything about us—our worth, significance, and value—comes from what we as individuals do, rather than from God.

There is another dimension to the power that comes with distinguishing between worth and worthiness. Even though they do not overlap, there is an important relationship between the two. The more we understand and have a testimony of the true source of our worth, the greater is our desire to be worthy. In other words, the more we trust in and appreciate Heavenly Father's love for us personally, the more we want to live His commandments. Jesus did not say He will love us IF we keep His commandments; He *did* say, "If you love me, keep my commandments" (John 14:15). When we trust in our divine worth, we can't help but feel God's love. This in turn engenders our love for Him. When we know we are precious to Heavenly Father and the Savior, we do not want to let Them down.

Even if we lose sight of our eternal worth and identity for a time, the reality of who we really are and how much we are really cherished is still present and waiting to be rediscovered. Even if some people have limited freedom because of incarceration or addiction, agency is still present. Even if we don't avail ourselves of Christ and all of the blessings of His Atonement, they are still available and beckoning to us. Moreover, we don't have to be at a certain level of worthiness to partake of the Atonement. The sooner we submit to the Atonement of Christ the happier and more richly blessed we will be. It will bless us throughout eternity in one way or another. The only question is how fully we will allow it to bless us. The question is not *if*, but *when* and *how much*.

God Loves Me, But Am I Supposed to Love Myself?

Some would have us believe that we are not supposed to like, let alone love, ourselves. They are misinterpreting the very essence of the first two commandments (see Matt. 22:37–39). First, we are to love God with all our heart; second, we are to love others as we love *ourselves*. Love is the essence of life. It hardly makes sense to love God and to love all other people who are children of God, and then not like or love ourselves.

What would cause us to think it is not good to value ourselves? Such thinking certainly starts with the adversary. Elder Neal A. Maxwell said, "Self-contempt is of Satan; there is none of it in heaven" (*Neal A. Maxwell Quote Book*, Cory H. Maxwell, ed. [Salt Lake City: Bookcraft, 2001], 306). While love comes to us by the grace of God, His very first commandment is to love Him back just as He loves us—with all our heart, might, mind, and strength. Again, as with all commandments, we are able to do that only through His grace. We are able to love Him "because He first loved us" (1 John 4:19). It is also through His grace that we are filled with the love to keep His second commandment, "Thou shalt love thy neighbor as thyself" (Matt. 22:39). Only through God's love

Love is the essence of life. It hardly makes sense to love God and all other people and then not love ourselves.

are we able to genuinely love others and *genuinely love ourselves*. Author Jonathan Chamberlain called the void that we feel when we do not experience God's love our empty love bucket. He explains that we are trying to fill this love bucket with things of the world that just cannot fill it. The only way to fill this love bucket is to receive God's love and, from Him, to feel a genuine gratitude to be who we are.

We are not talking about a selfish, inwardly focused obsession with ourselves that will shrink our souls and obscure our identity. We are not talking about any love that originates with us. That would not be charity. James MacArthur, highly successful psychologist and BYU professor, taught that each of us needs to feel significant, important, worthwhile, and valuable. This is not an ego trip. It only becomes an ego trip if you think you have more significance, importance, or are more worthwhile or valuable than others (see "The Functional Family," address given at the Family Expo Conference, Brigham Young University, April 2000).

> **Belief Window**
>
> Am I as gentle and patient with myself as I am with others?
>
> If not, why not?

When the Lord tells us to love our neighbors *as* ourselves, He is teaching that it is normal and foundational to love ourselves. Again, if we have a humble testimony of who we are, we are thankful to be who we are and we are happy being who we are—not because we created us but because a loving Heavenly Father created us. That understanding naturally helps us want others to likewise know who they are and to feel the same joy that we have. That is what it means to love our neighbor as we love ourselves. You can't share what you don't have, but when you have it, you can't help but share it. Those who don't truly love themselves as children of God cannot truly love others in the eternal way He intended. Without allowing the love of God into our hearts, we simply do not have the power to extend it to others.

This love for self might be more palatable to some when it is labeled *self-respect*. In writing about self-respect, Elder Neal A. Maxwell penned, "This is one of the great but underappreciated blessings of the restored gospel. It richly assures us of our intrinsic value and of our eternal and ultimate worth" (*Men and Women of Christ* [Salt Lake City: Bookcraft, 1991], 128). A testimony of the gospel should, in theory, bear the fruit of a healthy self-respect because the fruit of His Spirit is love (see Gal. 5:22). Even when we have sinned, the Spirit will not give us the feeling of hating ourselves but will give us a desire to be reconciled to God—and thus, better than we "naturally" are. It is Satan who influences us to hate ourselves when we have fallen short.

In practice, it takes time to conform our lives and our views to our testimonies, but in reality, only God's love can change our hearts. So when we don't feel good about ourselves, it may be because we need to seek the Spirit. And just as we gain a testimony that the restored gospel is true, we can likewise gain a testimony of who we are, collectively and individually.

> **Identity Check**
>
> "Can you imagine a more compelling motivation to worthwhile endeavor than the knowledge that you are a child of God, the Creator of the universe, our all-wise Heavenly Father who expects you to do something with your life and who will give help when help is sought for? Respect for self is the beginning of virtue in men. That man who knows that he is a child of God, created in the image of a divine Father and gifted with a potential for the exercise of great and godlike virtues, will discipline himself against the sordid, lascivious elements to which all are exposed."
>
> —President Gordon B. Hinckley, *Teachings of Gordon B. Hinckley* (Salt Lake City: Deseret Book, 1997), 158

"Grateful to Be Me"

The gratitude that accompanies such a testimony will help us be content with who we are and what the Lord has allotted us in this life. This testimony becomes a great motivation for disciplining ourselves and thereby honoring, by the lives we lead, the very being we are created to be. We will strive to "fill the measure of our creation" and become like Christ (see D&C 88:25). Consider the following life-changing, even miraculous experience that taught Barbara about the love and gratitude that can come only with a testimony of our worth and identity:

> From the time I was about eight years old, my father and mother supported me in athletic endeavors. Speed ice-skating was my major interest; I was quite successful throughout all the age group levels, which culminated in

my qualifying for the United States Olympic Speed Skating Team when I was a senior in high school. Throughout my twenties I competed internationally in the Olympics and world championships. I also did well in other things, such as academics and music.

Despite those successes, inside I was empty, lonely, and was basically addicted to negative self-talk. I liked what I could do, but was always extremely critical of myself. To get out of this rut of negative thinking, or to fill the void, I thought I just needed to accomplish great things. If I could do that, then maybe I would like myself. It never happened. No matter how great the accomplishments, nothing changed inside. There was no accompanying boost in self-esteem as I had anticipated.

Then it was my amazing fortune to be taught the gospel by the missionaries. I gained a testimony of the Prophet Joseph Smith, the truthfulness of the Book of Mormon, and the restored gospel of Jesus Christ and was baptized and confirmed a member of The Church of Jesus Christ of Latter-day Saints in between my first and second Olympic competitions. After about ten years of membership and ten more years of failing to fill the void within me, I turned to Heavenly Father in earnest prayer. "Father, do you love me? Can anyone love me?" He answered with a penetrating response: "Of course, I love you. You are my daughter."

After this I had a complete testimony of His love, but nothing changed. Why not? Why was I still so filled with negative self-talk instead of feeling how precious I was to Him? My heart needed to be changed and I could not do that myself. I knew Heavenly Father loved me, and I trusted that He would not leave me so lonely and despondent; I trusted that He could and would change my heart so that I would feel respect and gratitude for being who I am.

I earnestly prayed for about six months, constantly petitioning Heavenly Father to change my heart—to fill the void, so to speak. One day I was praying and I said, "Father, I am grateful to be me." I was stunned—did that come from me? Who said that? Yes, it was exactly how I felt. My tears flowed freely as I realized that Father had miraculously changed my heart and I was filled with gratitude to be me.

Before this, I do not remember feeling that way at any time in my entire life. In the thirty years since, I have never once gone back to the negative self-talk or the feelings of despair, no matter how difficult life became. I truly have never thirsted again and have always been filled.

This conversion of my heart from such negative feelings about myself to becoming grateful for exactly who I am was miraculous because it came from God. It came line upon line in a gradual manner. First Heavenly Father answered my pleading and allowed me to truly feel that He loves me. That did not automatically result in my liking myself. There had to be another step. The next step took a great deal of additional prayer and faith. I had the faith that Heavenly Father loved me and would not leave me in the mess I was in. I wanted to feel about my life as He did and I had faith that He would make that happen.

Prior to this change, the void I felt was devastating. It was a constant, ever-present loathing. It produced nothing but sorrow and sadness within. As I developed more trust in God's love for me, my faith that He would change me increased. I could not imagine that my loving Heavenly Father would want me to live with this horrible void and darkness. It was very apparent to me that only Heavenly Father could fill that void with love and that only He could change the darkness to light.

I know that He wants all of His children to be filled with His love by their turning to Him to fill any void that might be present. Only He can allow us to feel completely grateful for who we are: His children. When His love fills our being, it is such a contrast to being without that love, you cleave to it and never let it go. It is a most beautiful thing to experience. It is real, powerful, and lasting.

Some may think that such an experience would make us complacent; we would lose our motivation. In fact, just the opposite happens. Rather than complacency, there is a feeling of great peace. The void is filled and we can begin to move confidently forward. When we have a testimony that we are precious to Heavenly Father and to the Savior, we do not feel the need to look anywhere else for our worth, value, or importance. When we *really* know that we are precious to Heavenly Father, we do not want to disappoint Him. We do not want anything to come between us and Him. Therefore, we are filled with love for Him and for the Savior, and we want to live the commandments. Motivated by God's love, we want to do our best, look our best, and be our best. Those feelings are not motivated by the desire to *get* something but rather to *give* something.

When we feel love from Him and for Him, then we want to extend that love and the feelings of peace to others. We want to share our talents and edify, we want to lift and serve. Life becomes oriented to giving instead of to getting. When our love buckets are full of the love of God and the accompanying respect and gratitude for ourselves, we do not need to get something because we are filled. Now we can give, and give freely, not needing or expecting anything in return. According to President Dieter F. Uchtdorf, such a desire to give—especially to contribute to the happiness of others—is the true spirit of compassion (see "You Are My Hands," *Ensign*, May 2010, 70).

There will always be difficult and trying days when we feel rejected or are treated poorly by others. But people are not the wellspring of our worth. On those days, we do get hurt, get put down, feel sad, and cry. But those feelings do not last or control our lives unless we allow them to. We feel them, deal with them, and move on. The realization comes that behavior is not the source of our worth or value—not our behavior or the behavior of others. This is why we can do as Father commanded—love the sinner but not the sin (see Luke 6:32). We can love others even when they hurt us. Of course, we should never allow anyone to abuse us or cause us harm, but when we are secure in God's love it is easier to love others even when they treat us badly. Also, we continue to love ourselves even when we do not live up to our standards. If we continue to be firm but gentle with ourselves (as

---

Belief Window

Can I honestly tell the Lord that I am grateful to be me?

---

we would be with others), we will not harden our hearts and reject God's love. As President Uchtdorf described it, we will feel the love of our Father in Heaven even when we disobey (see Dieter F. Uchtdorf, "The Love of God," *Ensign*, Nov. 2009, 22). And that feeling motivates us to repent and get back on track.

Unfeigned Love and Gratitude *for* God

Love is at the very heart of our eternal identity. Our love and gratitude for God are at the heart of discovering and protecting that identity. God's love for us is unfeigned, meaning it is unforced, freely given, sincere, and genuine (see D&C 121:41–46). We must learn to love Him in this manner as well.

Losing everything he owned and all of his family except his wife, Job still declared, "Though he slay me, yet will I trust in Him" (Job 13:15) and "The Lord gave and the Lord hath taken away; blessed be the name of the Lord" (Job 1:21). We must learn to be a little more like Job—grateful for whatever lot He gives us in this life, knowing He is guiding us and has ordered everything for our eternal good. He has made it possible through the sacrifice of His Son to make everything come out right in the end. We will lack nothing if we submit gratefully to Him and His will.

Gratitude unlocks the door to loving God and loving ourselves. President Monson taught that gratitude helps us to feel the love of God (see "The Divine Gift of Gratitude," *Ensign*, Nov. 2010). Gratitude opens the eyes, the heart, the mind, and the spirit to see, understand, and glory in the truth of who we are—magnificent creatures of God. Let us be grateful for all that has been done in our behalf and grateful that we are on the way to exaltation instead of complaining about the bumps in the road that even now are moving us closer to our destiny. Let us love the Lord, love our lives, and love being who we are, warts and all.

How Does Faith in the Atonement Help Me Recover, Protect, and Fulfill My Identity?

THE ATONEMENT OF JESUS CHRIST, including the love that motivated it, is the key to understanding, embracing, and actualizing our identity. We could say it is identity theft insurance. In other words, losing our false "natural man" identity and becoming one with Christ—taking His name and nature upon us—is the only way to recognize and further claim our own eternal identity. That seems counterintuitive but only the Lord can show us the truth of who we are and make us what we have the potential to become. To the extent that we are in harmony with Christ and His Atonement, our identity is insured.

The Atonement of Jesus Christ, including the love that motivated it, is the key to understanding, embracing, and actualizing our identity.

When the Apostle Peter objected to the Lord washing his feet at the Last Supper, the Savior said to him, "If I wash thee not, thou hast no part with me" (John 13:8). Like Peter, we must serve the Master but we must also let Him serve us. His Atonement is His most important service to us; if we love Him and want to become like Him, we cannot let His ultimate sacrifice be offered to us in vain. We must invite Him to heal all of us, even the ugly and undesirable parts of our lives. He already knows them and has atoned for them anyway. We must hold nothing back as we acknowledge our sins and sinful nature. We must yield our hearts to Him and allow Him to wash them clean and make them new.

William Tyndale (A.D. 1484–1536) was the first to translate large portions of the Bible from Hebrew and Greek into English, a work for which he was later put to death. During his translation, Tyndale struggled to find an English word that would convey the meaning of the Hebrew word that described the great sacrifice and work that Christ performed in reconciling man to God. Not finding an English word that adequately expressed this concept, Tyndale made up a word—*at-one-ment*—to express the reuniting of mankind with God through His Son (see Richard N. Holzapfel, Dana M. Pike, and David R. Seely, *Jehovah and the World of the Old Testament* [Salt Lake City: Deseret Book, 2009], 119).

At the Last Supper, in addition to washing the feet of the Apostles, the Savior also prayed a last vocal prayer for them; both of these acts help us understand how our identity is linked to His. That prayer—recorded in John 17 and known as the Great Intercessory Prayer—was one in which the Lord was interceding with the Father for His disciples and for all of us as well. Jesus prayed that His disciples "may all be one; as thou, Father, art in me, and I in thee, that they also may be one in us" (John 17:21). In other words, Christ prayed that His "at-one-ment" would unite them with Him and His Father forever. When we become one with our Heavenly Father and Savior, we recover our real identity—a spiritual identity that Satan and the world seek to rob from us.

The Atoning Blood of Christ Completes Our Identity

We already took our first major step toward recovering, protecting, and fulfilling our eternal divine identity in the premortal world when we repented and exercised faith in the Atonement of Christ, casting our lot with Him and our Heavenly Father. In the book of Revelation we learn that we valiantly overcame Satan in the first estate "by the blood of the Lamb [the atonement], and by the word of [our] testimony; and [we] loved not [our] lives unto the death" (Rev. 12:11). We demonstrated by our choices and actions there that we believed Christ actually could and would carry out the Atonement and that it had the power to redeem, sanctify, and glorify us. Indeed, it had that power even before its earthly completion—our premortal sins and mistakes there were wiped away as if they had never happened. We now just have to prove that we continue to believe that the Atonement *was* accomplished and continues to have that same power. It's that simple.

We are not here to be perfect, though that is our ultimate goal through the Resurrection. But even that is made possible only through the Atonement of Christ. Rather, we show our faith and testimony here on earth just as we did in the life before—by our desires, thoughts, and actions; by repenting; by submitting our hearts and lives to Christ; by holding back nothing—

When we are saved and exalted, we will readily recognize and reverently confess that it is through the "merits of him who is mighty to save."

ing—"loving not our lives unto the death." When we are saved and exalted, we will readily recognize and reverently confess that it is through the "merits of him who is mighty to save" (2 Ne. 31:19) and not through any merit of our own in any way, shape, or form. Our works are simply tokens that demonstrate our gratitude and love for the Savior, our desires to receive His long-promised blessings, and our faith that His Atonement can restore our eternal identity by making us one with God again.

The Importance of Understanding the Atonement

As with the Nephites of old, learning more about the Atonement will help us exercise greater faith in it and enjoy more of its blessings. After King Benjamin taught the Nephites of their fallen condition and of the coming life and sacrifice of Jesus Christ that would redeem them, they fell to the earth because "they had viewed themselves in their own carnal state, even less than the dust of the earth" (Mosiah 4:2). The phrase *less than the dust of the earth* is not describing their lack of worth or identity, but rather teaching them that they have no ability to overcome the effects of spiritual death that come to us both because of Adam's transgression and our own sins. King Benjamin is teaching the people of his day and ours that we have no more ability than the dust of the earth to save ourselves from death and hell. We are all totally reliant upon the loving mercy of the Son of God.

Those who heard King Benjamin "cried aloud with one voice, saying: O have mercy, and apply the atoning blood of Christ that we may receive forgiveness of our sins, and our hearts may be purified; for we believe in Jesus Christ, the Son of God, who created heaven and earth, and all things; who shall come down among the children of men" (Mosiah 4:2). We must likewise come to see the reality of our fallen condition and learn how and why the atoning blood of Christ must be applied to our souls.

The Prophet Joseph Smith taught that the Atonement is at the center of our religion and that all other teachings are only "appendages" to it (see *Teachings of the Prophet Joseph Smith*, comp. Joseph Fielding Smith [Salt Lake City: Deseret Book, 1976], 121). The Atonement is not only the foundation and essence of our doctrine but also of our identity. It should be the center of our existence. In order to fully exercise faith in it we must understand it— what it is, why we need it, what it does for us, how it blesses us in every aspect of our lives, how we are nothing without it. The more we understand it, the more we can center our identity in it and be healed, cocooned, even swallowed up in its eternal power and blessings.

Though it is already completed, the Atonement is continuous, constant, and comprehensive—infinite and eternal (see Alma 34:10). No aspect of our existence is outside of its reach. We cannot atone for ourselves or for anyone else. We do not have the power nor are we expected to do it. We cannot add to it or take away from it. We can, however, learn what Christ has already taken care of and what He continues to do for us—and then we must decide how much to let it rectify, restore, and refine our lives.

As members of the Church we often artificially divide the Atonement of Christ into "unconditional" blessings (those that apply to all of Heavenly Father's children, such as redemption from the Fall of Adam and universal resurrection) and "conditional" blessings (those that depend on our faithfulness to Christ). Yet, as Elder Jeffrey R. Holland taught, we must remember that all of the blessings of the Atonement, conditional and unconditional, are available only through the grace of Christ—and that all of them are given freely instead of having to be earned (see "The Atonement of Jesus Christ," *Ensign*, March 2008, 36). What all of this means is that even the "conditional" part of the Atonement is not about us or what we do. It's still all about Him—what He does for us—His sacrifice, His love, His mercy, and His transforming grace. This life is our chance to give ourselves to Him. As we give ourselves wholly to His word and will, He will share with us as "joint-heirs" His honor, glory, and exaltation (see Rom. 8:17).

Understanding Faith and Works

Because Latter-day Saints believe that works are inextricably linked to faith in Christ, some mistakenly believe that we claim that we "earn" our way to heaven through works, creating in us an underlying "earning mentality"—both doctrinally and practically. This same "earning mentality" or paradigm (way of viewing the world) that traps us into feeling that we need to do something noteworthy or look a certain way to be important or to have worth can also distort our understanding of Christ's Atonement. When we view the Savior's Atonement from the "earning" outlook, we may convince ourselves that we have to save ourselves or even partly save ourselves. We get the idea that we do "all that we can do" (2 Ne. 25:23) and then Christ's Atonement makes up *only* for that which we cannot do ourselves. This kind of mistaken thinking relegates our Savior to merely bridging a gap or making up the difference of what we did not accomplish. We may have viewed the Atonement, figuratively speaking, like the diagram below.

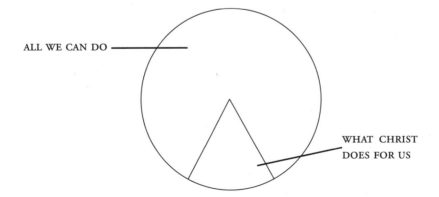

This greatly minimizes what the Savior has done for us and shows a lack of understanding about the true meaning of the Atonement. This perception has even been characterized by our critics as "the Lord of the Gap"—meaning that Mormons believe Jesus fills in only the small gaps that haven't been filled through our own diligence and hard work. Being sensitive to that criticism, we as Latter-day Saints seek to clarify that we DON'T believe that we can save ourselves and we DON'T view the Atonement merely as some kind of spiritual safety net. Unfortunately, we may still miss the point if our understanding of "all we can do" is reflected in this diagram:

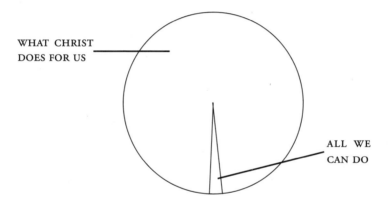

WHAT CHRIST
DOES FOR US

ALL WE
CAN DO

No matter how small we make the wedge of our works, this still is an incomplete understanding of the Atonement and of the role and love of Jesus Christ. Jesus's role is not merely a "majority" role or even an overwhelming contribution. It is an all-encompassing and consuming role. Without the Atonement of Christ, the whole plan collapses. Our opportunity to be here disappears. Our ability to develop and demonstrate faith is not possible. Our capacity to do good works comes only through His grace. We can do *nothing* without Him (see John 15:1–5; see also Moroni 7:24). King Benjamin explained specifically why this is so:

> I say unto you that if ye should serve him who has created you from the beginning, and is preserving you from day to day, by lending you breath, that ye may live and move and do according to your own will, and even *supporting you from one moment to another*—I say, if ye should serve

him with all your whole souls yet ye would be unprofitable servants.

And behold, all that he requires of you is to keep his commandments . . . therefore, if ye do keep his commandments he doth bless you and prosper you.

And now, in the first place, he hath created you, and granted unto you your lives, for which ye are indebted unto him.

And secondly, he doth require that ye should do as he hath commanded you; for which if ye do, he doth immediately bless you; and therefore he hath paid you. And ye are still indebted unto him, and are, and will be, forever and ever; therefore, *of what have ye to boast?* (Mosiah 2:21–24; emphasis added.)

Many other wonderful scripture passages make it clear that we *merit* nothing on our own:

"Wherefore, how great the importance to make these things known unto the inhabitants of the earth, that they may know that there is no flesh that can dwell in the presence of God, *save it be through the merits, and mercy, and grace of the Holy Messiah,* who layeth down his life according to the flesh, and taketh it again by the power of the Spirit, that he may bring to pass the resurrection of the dead, being the first that should rise" (2 Ne. 2:8; emphasis added).

"And now, my beloved brethren, after ye have gotten into this strait and narrow path, I would ask if all is done? Behold, I say unto you, Nay; for ye have not come thus far save it were by the word of Christ with unshaken faith in him, *relying wholly upon the merits of him who is mighty to save*" (2 Ne. 31:19; emphasis added).

"And since man had fallen *he could not merit anything of himself;* but the sufferings and death of Christ atone for their sins, through faith and repentance" (Alma 22:14; emphasis added).

"And if ye believe on his name ye will repent of all your sins, that thereby ye may have a remission of them through his merits" (Hel. 14:13; emphasis added).

"And after they had been received unto baptism, and were wrought upon and cleansed by the power of the Holy Ghost, they were numbered among the people of the church of Christ; and their names were taken, that they might be remembered and nourished by the good word of God, to keep them in the right way, to keep them continually watchful unto prayer, *relying alone upon the merits of Christ,* who was the author and the finisher of their faith" (Moroni 6:4; emphasis added).

"And that the Lamanites might come to the knowledge of their fathers, and that they might know the promises of the Lord, and that they may *believe the gospel and rely upon the merits of Jesus Christ,* and be glorified through faith in his name, and that through their repentance they might be saved. Amen" (D&C 3:20; emphasis added).

Perhaps the following diagram could illustrate our true relationship to Christ and His Atonement "after all we can do."

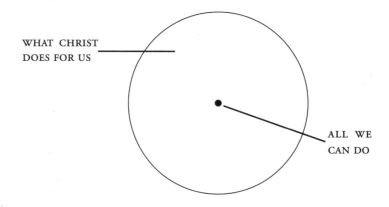

It may be that the "all we can do" is to "come unto Christ and be perfected *in* him" (Moroni 10:32), "encircled *around* in the robe of [His] righteousness" (2 Ne. 4:33), "encircled *about* eternally in the arms of his love [Atonement]" (2 Ne. 1:15), and "hid with Christ *in* God" (Col. 3:3.) Note how often in the scriptures, good things come to the righteous *in* Christ.

When we have faith unto repentance, we are "covered" (*kefar*)— protected from the punishment of eternal law and made whole in the embrace of our atoning redeemer (see Alma 34:16). His righteousness is imputed or credited to us (see Rom. 4). Only He can protect us from the consequences of the Fall of Adam and of our own personal fall. Only He can give us a new heart. Only through Him can we do good and become good. Only He can perfect and glorify us and present us pure before His Father. We supply our best effort through faith, repentance, and obedience to show that we desire His best, and He makes us new creatures *in* Him and like Him—at-one-ment.

So when Nephi earnestly tells us, "For we labor diligently to write, to persuade our children, and also our brethren, to believe in Christ, and to be reconciled to God; for we know that it is by grace that we are saved, after all we

> **Belief Window**
>
> Where do you see yourself in the circle of Christ's Atonement? Are you still trying to become perfect by yourself?

can do" (2 Nephi 25:23), we suggest that "all we can do" means doing the only thing that we are truly able to do on our own in this life: choosing to center our lives on Christ and His Atonement. Our choices and desires are the only thing we have control over and can offer to the Lord.

Accepting the atonement of Christ—or not—is all we personally are capable of in this life. We don't have the power to save ourselves. We don't even have the power on our own to do the works required of us, but we do have the ability to choose. As we desire to come unto Christ, we plant the seed that may become faith (see Alma 32). Christ grants us the gift of faith and enables us to do works that show our faith (see Eph. 2:8–10). He then rewards us for those efforts by increasing our faith.

Our hearts begin to change as we receive His Spirit and become a little more like Him, losing the desire to sin. We get answers to our greatest questions and increased knowledge of truth as we are obedient to God, promised President Monson (see "Obedience Brings Blessings," *Ensign*, May 2013). Our faith in and love for Him grows and we desire to do greater works. Through Christ our faith increases our works and our works increase our faith.

This is the eternal process of growth and perfection explained in Helaman: "Nevertheless they did fast and pray oft, and did wax stronger and stronger in their *humility*, and firmer and firmer in the *faith* of Christ, unto the filling their souls with joy and consolation, yea, even to the purifying and the sanctification of their hearts, which sanctification cometh [not because of great works but] because of their yielding their hearts unto God " (Hel. 3:35, emphasis added; see also D&C 93:13). The same process is also described in the Doctrine and Covenants: "That which is of God is light; and he that receiveth light [by choice], and continueth in God [by choice], receiveth more light; and that light groweth brighter and brighter until the perfect day" (D&C 50:24).

So thoroughly had the prophet Nephi, son of Helaman, participated in this process that the Lord granted him great power and a sort of independent identity: "And now, because thou hast done this with such unwearyingness, behold, I will bless thee forever; and *I will make thee mighty in word and in deed, in faith and in works*; yea, even that all things shall be done unto thee according to thy word, for thou shalt not ask that which is contrary to my will" (Hel. 10:5; emphasis added).

Again, it becomes obvious that we do not lose our identity or individuality by surrendering to Christ; we find it. President Ezra Taft Benson explained why this is so: "Men and women who turn their lives over to God will discover that He can make a lot more out of their lives than they can. He will deepen their joys, expand their vision, quicken their minds, strengthen their muscles, lift their spirits, multiply their blessings, increase their opportunities, comfort their souls, raise up friends, and pour out peace" ("Jesus Christ—Gifts and Expectations," *Ensign*, Dec. 1988, 2).

The Atonement Can Heal Everything

Under the law of Moses the Lord commanded the children of Israel to offer sacrifices in similitude of His coming Atonement. Sacrifices were offered not only for intentional sins but also for transgressions committed in ignorance, inadvertently or unintentionally (see Lev. 4, 5:1–13). They were also offered in behalf of people who were cleansed of diseases or who became ritually impure (see Lev. 12, 14). Such offerings served in part as symbols for the Israelites of the countless things in addition to sin that make mortals unworthy of the presence of God. All of these sacrifices seem to suggest that the Lord is keenly aware of the impurities that come to us simply by reason of living in a fallen world and that keep us from becoming like our Heavenly Father.

Thus, our sins and sinful nature are not all that can be healed and changed through the Atonement. As we have pointed out, nothing is beyond its reach, for it is the undergirding power behind our very existence here. It can heal, change, or make tolerable—and in most cases, even joyful—any defect in this life if we have faith in Christ and submit to Him. Because of His Atonement, even the most unthinkable and unjust situations can one day not only be wiped away or made right but also become a great blessing in realizing our eternal identity. This sure hope gives us strength to endure and prosper spiritually.

We need not feel that anything in our lives is our responsibility alone, our problem alone, or beyond the healing hand of the Great Physician. All of those things that keep us from optimizing our identity as children of a God and King can eventually be swept out of our lives: pride, insecurity, perfectionism, self-pity, a need for control, fear—and everything else, including things we may not have thought of!

We need not feel that anything in our lives is our problem alone or is beyond the healing hand of the Great Physician.

Referring to the Savior, we are told, "And he will take upon him death, that he may loose the bands of death which bind his people; and he will take upon him their infirmities, that his bowels may be filled with mercy, according to the flesh, that he may know according to the flesh how to succor his people according to their infirmities" (Alma 7: 12). Christ can heal these things because He has experienced them Himself. He understands the pain and He knows the way to deal with it. He knows what adjustments will make it better or easier to bear. He knows what will comfort us. He has the incomparable power of love and healing. It is really just a matter of our fully recognizing it and exercising the faith to access it, the humility to submit to it, and the patience to let it do its holy work. We will address the more practical aspects of how we might do this in chapter 7.

One final thought: We can't save the Savior any suffering by using only a little bit of the Atonement or by utilizing it only for our "big sins." The more we partake of and appreciate the Atonement in all aspects of our lives, the happier it makes Him. The last thing we want to do is try to go through this difficult mortal life alone or without the full range of help and mercy that could make it so much easier, happier, and more productive. Sooner or later—and the timing is up to us—we must yield everything to Him, or His efforts on our behalf will be in vain. To recover, protect, and fulfill our true identity we must have our whole souls thoroughly washed in His blood. "There can no man be saved except his garments are washed white; yea, his garments must be purified until they are cleansed from all stain, through the blood of him of whom it has been spoken by our fathers, who should come to redeem his people from their sins" (Alma 5:21). Or, as Christ Himself said, "If I wash thee not, thou hast no part with me" (John 13:8).

How Do I Entrust My Identity to Christ?

Trusting in the Atonement of Jesus Christ is sure protection against identity theft. The more fully we give ourselves to Him, the more of our identity we find and the more we find that our identity is completely tied up in Him. Submission to Him allows Him do the sanctifying work He sacrificed Himself to do for us. To allow Him to do this for us, we must *choose* to come unto Christ and surrender ourselves to Him—the only action we are truly capable of on our own in this life. It all boils down to individual choice.

Learning to submit ourselves to Christ and His Atonement is the simple answer to all of our problems as well as all our possibilities. It may be a simple answer but it is not an easy accomplishment. The teachings are plain but the application requires lifelong perseverance and inspired guidance. Anyone who truly desires to do it can "come boldly unto the throne of grace, that [they] may obtain mercy, and find grace to help in time of need" (Heb. 4:16).

> **Identity Check**
>
> "When we allow our will to be swallowed up in the will of the Father (Mosiah 15:7) then and only then do we 'see things as they really are and as they really will be' (Jacob 4:13). . . . Then we can receive submissively His direction and influence upon us. There is no other way."
>
> —Elder Neal A. Maxwell, *That Ye May Believe* (Bookcraft, 1992), 119–120

Self-perfection is not the goal. The goal is to demonstrate our desires and loyalty to the Lord as clearly as possible. The goal is to get pointed in the right direction in this life. The goal is to learn to rely wholly upon the merits of Christ. The goal is to "practice virtue and holiness before [Him]" (D&C 38:24)—with the emphasis on *practice*! How important it is, then, to spend our lives learning and applying the doctrine of the Atonement. Here are some practical things we can remember and do as we learn about the Atonement in our lives.

Anyone Can Do It

Sometimes we look at the Savior, prophets and apostles, and other general and local Church leaders, whether we know them personally or not, and think, "I'll never be able to be like them." That may be true in this life but it is not true in eternity. One day we will catch up to them if we are faithful. They may have advantages that we don't have in this life because more is required of them, but perfect is perfect and anyone who sincerely wants to be perfected in Christ may be so. Elder Sterling W. Sill implied this when he taught that "there is everything in knowing our origin and possible destiny. . . . God, angels, spirits, and men are all of the same species in different stages of righteousness and development" (Conference Report, Oct. 1965, 57).

No matter how good Church leaders are, not one can ever be perfect without Christ. Someday we will all be just as perfect as He is because that is what He unselfishly offers to do for us. At the funeral of fellow general authority Elder S. Dilworth Young of the Seventy, Elder Bruce R. McConkie taught that if we leave this life being faithful to our covenants and doing the best we can, it is the same as having our calling and election made sure, no matter how far along the road we have progressed:

> If we die in the faith, that is the same thing as saying that our calling and election has been made sure and that we will go on to eternal reward hereafter. As far as faithful members of the church are concerned, they have charted a course leading to eternal life. As far as faithful people are concerned, if they are in line of their duty, if they are doing what they ought to do, although they may not have been perfect in this sphere, their probation is ended. . . . It is true as the Prophet Joseph Smith said, that there are many things that have to be done "even beyond the grave" to work out our salvation, but we'll stay in the course and we will not alter from it, if we have been true and faithful in this life.

Likewise, Hugh Nibley insightfully observed:

> Who is righteous? Anyone who is repenting. No matter how bad he has been, if he is repenting, he is a righteous man. There is hope for him. And no matter how good he has been all his life, if he is not repenting, he is a wicked man. The difference is which way you are facing. The man on the top of the stairs facing down is much worse off than the man on the bottom step who is facing up. The direction we are facing, that is repentance; and this is what determines whether we are good or bad. ("Funeral Address, Approaching Zion," *Collected Works of Hugh Nibley* [Salt Lake City: Deseret Book, 1989], 9:301–302)

This is the principle the Lord Himself tried to teach His disciples in the parable recorded in Matthew 20:1–15. This parable, often called the parable of the workers in the vineyard, teaches us that we don't have to be at a certain level of righteousness to have access to the love and enabling power of Christ. We start wherever we are, and the eventual reward is the same for everyone. "Even if ye can no more than desire to believe," as the prophet Alma

> **Belief Window**
>
> Do you believe that you can be forgiven of your sins?
>
> Do you believe that Christ can make you whole?

taught, "let this desire work in you" (Alma 32:27). Alma knew this from personal experience. His desire sprang from desperation born of exquisite suffering for his sins. Only then did he care to remember his father's teachings about Jesus Christ, the Son of God, who would atone for the sins of the world. When his "mind caught hold upon this thought, [he] cried within [his] heart: O Jesus, thou Son of God, have mercy on me[!]" (Alma 36:17–18). He not only found immediate relief, but he experienced joy that was as exquisite as his suffering. Of course, a demonstration of his sincerity had to follow, but the beginning of access to Christ's Atonement can be as close as one righteous thought, one sincere desire, one earnest prayer.

President Boyd K. Packer declared that except for defection to perdition after having known a fullness, no other sin or rebellion or addiction is exempt from forgiveness. When we sincerely desire it and are willing to pay the "uttermost farthing," our sins and rebellions and addictions are transferred to the Lord, and He settles our accounts in a way that we with our mortal understanding cannot comprehend (see "The Brilliant Morning of Forgiveness," *Ensign*, Nov. 1995, 19–20). This is the comforting doctrine of the Atonement.

Educate Our Desires

Desire is the obvious first step. Elder Neal A. Maxwell taught that our desires are the root of our actions. He emphasized how we are not at the mercy of uncontrollable urges, but that we have the power to "educate" and train our desires:

> *Desire* denotes a real longing or craving. Hence righteous desires are much more than passive preferences or fleeting feelings. Of course our circumstances and environments matter very much, and they shape us significantly. Yet there remains an inner zone in which we are sovereign, unless we abdicate. In this zone lies the essence of our individuality and our personal accountability.
>
> Therefore, what we insistently desire, over time, is what we will eventually become and what we will receive in eternity. "For I [said the Lord] will judge all men according to their works, according to the desire of their hearts" (D&C 137:9; see also Jer. 17:10). Alma said, "I know that [God] granteth unto men according to their desire, . . . I know that he allotteth unto men . . . according to their wills" (Alma 29:4).
>
> Even a spark of desire can begin change. ("According to the Desire of [Our] Hearts," *Ensign*, Nov. 1996, 21)

If our righteous desires are weak or we still struggle with unrighteous desires that wear down our resolve to do better, we can at the very least pray to God and express a desire to be better. We can continually acknowledge our own helplessness without Him and plead with the Lord to change our hearts. This is the beginning of faith, the planting of the seed. After we express our desires, faith comes to us as a gift from God. Notice how God grants us the power to have and exercise faith:

> Therefore may God *grant* unto you, my brethren, that ye may begin to exercise your faith unto repentance, that ye

begin to call upon his holy name, that he would have mercy upon you; . . .

Yea, and it came to pass that the Lord our God did visit us with assurances that he would deliver us; yea, insomuch that he did speak peace to our souls, and did grant unto us great faith, and did cause us that we should hope for our deliverance in him. (Alma 34:17; Alma 58: 11, emphasis added)

As our faith and prayers increase, we can begin to add outward actions, one at a time if necessary. Elder Maxwell further encouraged us: "Each assertion of a righteous desire, each act of service, and each act of worship, however small and incremental, adds to our spiritual momentum. Like Newton's Second Law, there is a transmitting of acceleration as well as a contagiousness associated with even the small acts of goodness" ("According to the Desire of [Our] Hearts," *Ensign*, November 1996, 21).

Yielding Our Identity to Christ

Once we have obtained the desire to come unto Christ and be perfected in Him (see Moroni 10:31) and we begin to exercise faith and practice obedience, the process of change begins. We begin to recover our true identity. That identity is no less than becoming exactly like Jesus Christ, but how does this happen?

Contrary to popular opinion, this is not the phase of our existence where we indulge our own interests and seek our own identity. This is not the time to heedlessly pursue our own dreams and desires—to seek power, honor, and material reward from mankind—although that is exactly what the world is telling us we should do. These things are not guaranteed for

> Once we desire to come unto Christ and begin to exercise faith and practice obedience, we begin to recover our true identity—no less than becoming exactly like Jesus Christ.

this life because they are not what really matters. In this life the only guarantee is that the Lord will bless us and help us triumph if we are faithful.

Sometimes we unwisely create for ourselves scenarios we expect our lives to follow or identities and roles we expect to realize. Someone once said, "Expectations are frustrations waiting to happen." How much unnecessary pain and suffering do we cause ourselves and others because we expect that life will turn out the way we envision? How much time do we waste fighting the Lord's true will for us by being frustrated and angry that our life is not going the way we expected? How much energy do we expend trying to be someone we are not?

No one is promised that he will have an easy life and all his dreams will come true. No one is promised that her life will be ideal or will go just as she desires it to go. We are blessed just to be here and have a body! That, along with the saving ordinances, is the only thing on this earth that is absolutely essential to our salvation. Everything else that we get to experience and learn is frosting on the cake!

> **Belief Window**
>
> Do you believe that Christ has the power to make you just like Him?

All guarantees of rest, reward, glory, power, eternal families, and freedom to fulfill our righteous dreams are realized in the next life if our lives have been "living sacrifices," as the Apostle Paul characterized righteousness, in similitude of Christ's sacrifice for us (see Rom. 12:1). He asks this of us because this is what was required of Him:

> Let this mind be in you, which was also in Christ Jesus:
> Who, being in the form of God, thought it not robbery to be equal with God:
> But *made himself of no reputation*, and took upon him the form of a servant, and was made in the likeness of men:
> And being found in fashion as a man, he humbled *himself*, and became obedient unto death, even the death of the cross.
> Wherefore God also hath highly exalted him, and given him a name which is above every name:
> That at the name of Jesus every knee should bow, of things in heaven, and things in earth, and things under the earth;

And that every tongue should confess that Jesus Christ *is* Lord, to the glory of God the Father. (Philip. 2:5–11; emphasis added.)

Christ gave His life countless times and in countless ways. He gave up the glorious and powerful life He enjoyed with His Father in the premortal world and came to earth. He did nothing on earth according to His own will but dedicated His entire life to doing His Father's will. Finally, He gave up His mortal life to ransom His Father's children from sin and death. Even in His current glorified, exalted state, His life is not about Himself but about doing the will of His Father in providing immortality and eternal life to others.

Likewise, this life is not about us—it is about identifying ourselves with Christ and serving Him, giving Him all the credit. When we follow His example and give our lives for Him, we will enjoy the same reward He enjoys, though surely we will always be indebted to Him as our Savior and King.

> # This life is not about us—it is about identifying ourselves with Christ and serving Him, giving Him all the credit.

Christ Is Our Identity in This Life

The scriptures clearly teach us that we should seek to have the identity of Christ to be identified as fully as possible with Him. We are to take upon us the name of Christ (see Moroni 4:3), to seek to have His image in our countenance (see Alma 5:19), to seek to have the mind of Christ (see 1 Cor. 2:16), to become like Him so that when he appears we shall be like Him (see Moroni 7:48). We are commanded to let our light so shine that it may glorify not us, but our Father in Heaven (see Matt. 5:16). Christ further clarified that we should hold up His light, not our own (see 3 Ne. 18:24). Accordingly, He asks us to give up, or give our lives and identity, to Him:

"And he said to *them* all, If any *man* will come after me, let him deny himself, and take up his cross daily, and follow me.

"For whosoever will save his life shall lose it: but whosoever will lose his life for my sake, the same shall save it.

Identity Check

"We want to be . . . fit companions of the Gods and Holy Ones. In an organized capacity we can assist each other in not only doing good but in refining ourselves, and whether few or many come forward and help to prosecute this great work, they will be those that will fill honorable positions in the Kingdom of God. . . . Women [and men] should be women [and men] and not babies that need petting and correction all the time. I know we like to be appreciated but if we do not get all the appreciation [and other worldy rewards] which we think is our due, what matters? We know the Lord has laid high responsibility upon us, and there is not a wish or desire that the Lord has implanted in our hearts in righteousness but will be realized, and the greatest good we can do to ourselves and each other is to refine and cultivate ourselves in everything that is good and ennobling to qualify us for those responsibilities."

—Eliza R. Snow

"For what is a man advantaged, if he gain the whole world, and lose himself, or be cast away?" (Luke 9:23–25.)

What does it mean to lose our life for His sake? It doesn't mean we become a doormat or give up control of our own will! It does not mean debasing ourselves, disrespecting ourselves, or diminishing ourselves. It is not being servile to please others or to get our identity and recognition from pleasing others.

It *does* mean that we willingly and purposely and daily take His name and His image and His identity upon us and do as He asks. It *does* mean that we stubbornly maintain our independence from the world while at the same time yielding our hearts to the Lord. It *does* mean that we spend our time, talents, and energy serving Him and His cause and letting Him make of us what He will. It *does* mean that when we take time for ourselves, it is only so that we can strengthen ourselves to serve Him better.

Losing our lives for His sake also means losing or surrendering the world's and our own distorted vision of our identity. We do this in at least three ways:

First, we must give up the honors of men. We must learn to not fear men or value their opinions more than the opinions and approval of God. We must give up the need for material things or worldly pleasures and applause to give us worth or identity. These things are not the source of our true identity. They cannot give it, change it, fulfill it, or take it away, but they can obscure our understanding, appreciation, and achievement of our true worth and identity. "The cares of the world are so many and so entangling," President Spencer W. Kimball cautioned, "even very good people are diverted from following the truth because they care too much for the things of the world" ("Listen to the Prophets," *Ensign*, May 1978, 77).

The Savior inquired of the recognition-driven Pharisees, "How can ye believe, which receive honour one of another, and seek not the honour that *cometh* from God

We must learn to not value the opinions of men more than the opinions and approval of God.

only?" (John 5:44). The world's treasures and approbation cannot give us faith, hope, charity, forgiveness of sins, or any of the other gifts that come only through trusting in the Atonement of Christ. They cannot fit us for our Father's kingdom. There is no longer time to waste even window shopping the merchandise of the world. Remember that, like Jesus, "[our] kingdom is not of this world" (John 18:36).

Dawdling along on our way to the tree of life is more dangerous than it has ever been and there is a great responsibility that has been laid upon us. Let's step out of the so-called "gray areas" and be safely in the Lord's territory. We must be about our Father's work. It is time to stop worrying what others may think of us or that we may miss out on all the fun. When we finally and fully cast our lot with Christ, we begin to see that the world has nothing of lasting value to offer us and we must be on our way. The Apostle Paul stated it bluntly when he said, "I count all things but loss for the excellency of the knowledge of Christ Jesus my Lord: for whom I have suffered the loss of all things, and *do count them but dung*, that I may win Christ" (Philip. 3:8; emphasis added). Do you know what dung is? Enough said!

Second, we must give our problems and pains to Christ. Not only must we give away all our sins to know Him (see Alma 22:18), we must make a decision to turn our weaknesses, trials, disappointments, and deficiencies over to Christ. This is the very purpose of the Atonement—to help us use the negatives of mortality as steppingstones and turn them into positives. Our sufferings are an important part of our unique identity. Our adversities are gifts intended to shape and sharpen our true identity *if* we follow Christ with firm faith and a fixed determination to serve Him. He will show us how they will help make us what we are intended to be both here and hereafter. So often we find our life's calling in overcoming a weakness, making it a strength through the Atonement of Christ, and setting an example for others to follow.

> Our adversities are gifts intended to sharpen our true identity; if we follow Christ with firm faith, He will show us how they will help make us what we are intended to be both here and hereafter.

"Come unto me, all ye that labour and are heavy laden," the Savior implored us, "and I will give you rest. Take my yoke upon you, and learn of me; for I am meek and lowly in heart: and ye shall find rest unto your souls. For my yoke is easy, and my burden is light" (Matt. 11:28–30).

"Cast thy burden upon the Lord," advised the psalmist, "and he shall sustain thee: he shall never suffer the righteous to be moved" (Ps. 55:22). Trusting Him with our burdens is a conscious choice that requires faith and continual *practice*. In return we *practice* taking His burden upon us—doing the best we can to live His gospel—for His yoke is easy and His burden is light (see Matt. 11:30). It is something uncomplicated that we can manage. Nevertheless, it also takes a lifetime of *practice* to learn to trust Him to heal and perfect us. Trying to be in control and obsessing about our own problems transfers them back to our shoulders, where they can run us into the ground and drive us to despair. The sooner we learn this, the happier we will be.

How does this work in practical terms? We may not know just how to overcome a problem in our lives that could be healed by the Atonement. We alone may not have the strength or understanding. We might even make things worse trying to fix it on our own. We certainly make anything worse when we obsess about it. But we do know how to pray, how to read scriptures (even if we don't fully understand them), how to attend church meetings, how to partake of the sacrament, how to attend the temple, how to give service, and how to pay tithing, among other things. In other words, we know countless ways that we can lose ourselves by taking the easy yoke of Christ upon us while transferring our own complicated burdens and imperfections to Him.

Keeping the Savior's simple and gentle commandments demonstrates that we have faith in His ability to change our hearts and ease our burdens, to make us whole and perfect in Him. We submit to Him by doing His will while putting aside our own self-centered desires, problems, and obsessions. He heals us as we serve Him; we don't have to heal ourselves! That doesn't mean that we don't have to do all we can to work through our challenges; it *does* mean that after we do all we can, we leave them confidently in His hands.

As we noted, transferring our negatives to the Lord sounds easy but it takes practice and discipline. How do we do it? An old parable illustrates this principle so well that it is worth repeating here. This parable has been told in many different forms and versions but the important lesson is still the same. We'll use the Old Indian version. A young brave whose father was the chief of his Indian tribe was continually getting into trouble and bringing disgrace upon his tribe, his father, and his family. One day after a disgraceful display of poor judgment, the chief of the tribe confronted his willful son.

"Why do you continue to do these things that bring such shame upon your people?" asked the chief in frustration.

Hanging his head, the son replied, "I want to stop doing these things. I know they are wrong. I want to make better choices but it is as if there are two dogs fighting within me. One is a good dog and one is a bad dog. Each time the fight between them is terrible but the bad dog always wins. What am I to do?" the brave inquired helplessly.

Looking his son in the eye, the chief solemnly advised, "Feed the right dog!"

In other words, strengthen the dog you want to win. Every desire and act of righteousness, no matter how small, feeds our righteous desires and our faith in Christ's Atonement. If we continue to feed our better, positive nature, not only will the "man of Christ" (Hel. 3:29) begin to win, the natural man within us will eventually become weak and ultimately, through Christ, will starve to death! We can follow the example of our Savior when He said, speaking of food, "My meat is to do the will of him that sent me and to finish his work" (John 4:34). His mind was constantly filled with thoughts of glorifying His Father.

> **Belief Window**
>
> Do you believe that you can control your thoughts—even self-defeating thoughts and feelings of self-contempt?

An extremely important part of feeding the right dog is controlling the thoughts we allow to fill our minds and become part of our beliefs and desires. Here is the control center of our lives, of our eternal destiny! "As a man thinketh in his heart, so is he" (Prov. 23:7). Barbara has related how she received the profound testimony of her individual worth and never again doubted. Because of her faith and humility, the Lord has made "weak things become strong" unto her (see Ether 12:27). Her life's mission has been tied up in sharing this message with others.

We noted that most of us know this in theory but often forget it in practice. What is the difference? Why didn't Barbara struggle with ongoing doubts like most of us usually do? It isn't because she was never tempted. In fact, she was sorely tested by a series of painful personal setbacks that would have caused the strongest of us to question our value to the Lord. Doubts did come, but she refused to allow them to stay in her mind. Instead, she applied the mental discipline she had practiced for many years as an elite athlete to help her keep her focus. She continually reminded herself of the things she had felt and the testimony she had gained. She looked to the true source of her worth for messages about her worth. She not only weathered the storm but became even more convinced of the Lord's love for her as she saw that in the long run, her setbacks actually moved her forward.

The Prophet Joseph Smith also learned this difficult lesson in his life. "Let virtue garnish thy thoughts unceasingly," the Lord admonished the Prophet Joseph Smith as he languished in Liberty Jail (D&C 121:45). We too often confine the word *virtue* to sexual purity—but surely Joseph's struggle in the depths of despair was not with immoral thoughts but with discouragement, depression, self-doubt, and a temptation to question the Lord, his prophetic mission, and possibly even his own worth.

The original meaning of *virtue* was "strength" or "power." Imagine what a difference it would make in your life to let the "strength" or "power" of God "garnish [your] thoughts unceasingly!" The difference will be that your "confidence [will] wax strong in the presence of God" (D&C 121:45). In other words, you will become more and more confident of your identity as a child of the Most High and more confident of His love for you. Your faith and hope in Him, and therefore in yourself, will increase to the point where you can stand confidently in His presence without embarrassment or shame, and this because of the Atonement of Jesus Christ.

As we do this, our confidence and trust in His purposes for our lives likewise grows until, through our hope in Christ, we can overcome any negatives—including our thoughts, for it is in our thoughts that the descisive struggle with Satan plays out. It has been wisely said that "the greatest battles of life are fought daily in the silent chambers of the soul."

> As you let the strength of God garnish your thoughts unceasingly, you will become more and more confident of your identity as a child of the Most High.

Nephi spoke for many of us when he exclaimed, "Awake, my soul! No longer droop in sin. Rejoice, O my heart, and give place no more for the enemy of my soul" (2 Ne. 4:28).

As we mentioned earlier, one of the most powerful methods we can use to control our thoughts is to *practice* gratitude. Gratitude blesses everything it touches, while self-pity is poison. Gratitude therapy is so effective that it is becoming a legitimate recognized therapy in treating mental and emotional illness. There is no doubt that it would also aid in physical healing. It has the power to help us discover our true identity. Ingratitude keeps us from realizing and rejoicing in who we really are. It keeps us obsessed with ourselves, while gratitude makes us want to reach out to the Lord and to others.

Another effective way to control our thinking and feed the right dog is to garnish our thoughts with "the virtue of the word of God" (Alma 31:5). Continually feasting on the word of God fills our minds with light, truth, and strength, and leaves less room and energy for negative thoughts. The focus of the scriptures and teachings of the prophets as well as the teachings of the temple is Jesus Christ and His Atonement. Since our identity and our existence here are completely wrapped up in His Atonement, we would do well to study it continually.

Educating our desires, exercising faith, controlling our thoughts, and feeding our eternal identity are basic to immersing ourselves in the Atonement of Jesus Christ and recognizing who we are and what we can do. When our hearts are changed, the necessary actions will follow more easily. We will yield more readily to the power of the Atonement, to Jesus Christ Himself. As President Ezra Taft Benson put it, "When obedience ceases to be an irritant and becomes our quest, in that moment God will endow us with power" (quoted by Elder Donald L. Staheli, "Obedience—Life's Great Challenge," *Ensign*, May 1998, 82).

Third, we must give our very souls to Christ. In the Book of Mormon, the prophet Amaleki guarantees with an oath ("as the Lord liveth") that if we "offer [our] whole souls as an offering" to our Savior, we will be saved—exalted (Omni 1:26). On the other hand, we can infer that if we hold something back, He cannot save us. At some point we must be able to let go of everything that is not part of the eternal identity the Lord intends to help us realize. The sooner we do this, the happier and more powerful we are. We don't have to wait for a distant day to make that commitment. We can decide now, today, and cast our lot with the Lord. Consider the example set by President Boyd K. Packer, as related by President Ezra Taft Benson:

> Christ's great gift to us was His life and sacrifice. Should that not then be our small gift to Him—our lives and sacrifices, not only now but in the future? A few years ago my colleague Elder Boyd K. Packer said this: "I'm not ashamed to say that … I want to be good. And I've found in my life that it has been critically important [to establish this intention] between me and the Lord so that I knew that he knew which way I committed my agency. I went before Him and said, 'I'm not neutral, and you can do with me what you want. If you need my vote, it's there. I don't care what you do with me,

and you don't have to take anything from me because I give it to you—everything, all I own, all I am—,' and that makes the difference" ("To Those Who Teach in Troubled Times," address delivered at seminary and institute conference, Summer 1970, Salt Lake City). ("Jesus Christ—Gifts and Expectations," *Ensign*, Dec 1988, 2)

When we become members of the Lord's Church, we make our own oath or covenant with the Lord. It is only a matter of whether we will keep our word. If we have made temple covenants, we have further committed ourselves formally to give all that we have and are to the Lord. Again, the question is whether we really mean it. If we withhold ourselves from Christ, He cannot heal, change, or remake us in His image. Only when we offer our whole souls to Him can He make us whole. C. S. Lewis, the great Christian apologist, insightfully described how this "total makeover" must happen to each of us who want to realize our divine potential:

> And now we begin to see what it is that the New Testament is always talking about. It talks about Christians "being born again"; it talks about them "putting on Christ"; about Christ "being formed in us"; about our coming to "have the mind of Christ."
>
> Put right out of your head the idea that these are only fancy ways of saying that Christians are to read what Christ said and try to carry it out—as a man may read what Plato or Marx said and try to carry it out. They mean something much more than that. They mean that a real Person, Christ, here and now, in that very room where you are saying your prayers, is doing things to you. It is not a question of a good man who died two thousand years ago. It is a living Man, still as much a man as you, and still as much God as He was when He created the world, really coming and interfering with your very self; killing the old natural self in you and replacing it with the kind of self He has. At first, only for moments. Then for longer periods. Finally, if all goes well, turning you permanently into a different sort of thing; into a new little Christ, a being which, in its own small way, has the same kind of life as God; which shares in His power, joy, knowledge and eternity.

I have been talking as if it were we who did everything. In reality, of course, it is God who does everything. We, at most, allow it to be done to us. (*Mere Christianity* [New York: Harper Collins, 1980], 191)

In the Master's parable of the talents (see Matt. 25:14–30), there seems to be inequity between the servants because one is given five talents, another is given two talents, and the last is given only one talent. Each is expected to multiply those talents. Notice, however, that the servant with two talents is not expected to produce ten or even five. The servant who was given five talents and the servant who was given two talents both doubled their Lord's investment—a 100 percent return. This implies that both gave 100 percent—all they had—even though the investments and the outcomes were quantitatively different. Because the quality of their effort was the same, both received the same commendation and reward. We suspect that if the servant who was given one talent had put it to use and given his all—100 percent, doubling his talent to two talents—he too would have received the same blessing. The point is not what we are given but how much effort we give back—what we become as a result of what we do with what we are given.

> A real Person—Christ, here and now, in the very room where you are saying your prayers—is doing things to you.

On a far grander scale than we are capable of understanding, the Savior gave 100 percent of Himself for us, and that is what He asks of us in our sphere. We must give our all for Him so that we may one day hear Him say, "Well done, thou good and faithful servant: thou hast been faithful over a few things, I will make thee ruler over many things: enter thou into the joy of thy lord" (Matt. 25:21).

"In Your Patience Possess Ye Your Souls" (Luke 21:19)
Though a decision and a covenant to lose ourselves for Christ's sake can be made at one point in time, this surrendering and allowing takes a

lifetime of practice and more. Even the Lord Himself in this life "received not of the fulness at the first, but received grace for grace" and "continued from grace to grace, until he received a fulness" (D&C 93:12–13). He also learned obedience through suffering (see Heb. 5:8) like the rest of us do if we are teachable.

Learning from suffering implies experiencing pain and difficulty for an extended time until the necessary lesson is impressed deeply enough to do its work. Only God can determine when that process is truly complete, since only He understands perfection. It took time for Christ to experience His full, true identity on earth. This is symbolic for us. The Prophet Joseph taught this encouraging doctrine: "The nearer man approaches perfection, the clearer are his views, and the greater his enjoyments, till he has overcome the evils of his life and lost every desire for sin; and like the ancients, arrives at that point of faith where he is wrapped in the power and glory of his Maker and is caught up to dwell with Him. *But we consider that this is a station to which no man ever arrived in a moment*" (*Teachings of the Prophet Joseph Smith,* comp. Joseph Fielding Smith [Salt Lake City: Deseret Book, 1976], 51; emphasis added). Thus part of surrendering our souls to the Lord is surrendering to His timing as well as to His methods and His wisdom.

Will I Lose My Individuality?

Many are afraid to conform to the teachings of the gospel because they fear they will lose their unique identity as an individual. They disdain to follow anyone but, again ironically, in striking out on their own they become clones of countless other lost or rebellious souls in the world who are enslaved by the devil. The Lord continually warns us that if we are not for Him, we are against Him. There is no middle ground.

Without Christ and His Atonement to protect our identity, we become relegated to Satan's tragically restricting, repetitious, and unoriginal patterns of evil. "Show me one principle that has originated by the power of the Devil," President Brigham Young challenged. "You cannot do it. I call evil inverted good, or a correct principle made an evil use of." On the other hand he said, "That which is of God is pure, lovely, holy and full of all excellency and truth, no matter where it is found, in hell, in heaven, upon the earth, or in the planets" (*Discourses of Brigham Young,* John A. Widtsoe, comp. [Salt Lake City: The Church of Jesus Christ of Latter-day Saints, 1977], 69.)

"There is more individuality in those who are more holy," Elder Neal A. Maxwell observed. "Sin, on the other hand, brings sameness; it shrinks us to addictive appetites and insubordinate impulses" ("Repentance," *Ensign*, Nov. 1991, 30.) For those who reject Christ, individuality is limited to what Satan and *this* life can furnish them. In the next life, that means they are left with little or nothing to commend or distinguish them. As for those who yield to Christ, "Eye hath not seen, nor ear heard, neither have entered into the heart of man, the things which God hath prepared for them that love him" (1 Cor. 2:9).

The possibilities and variations are endless and unlimited. The great irony of surrendering our will to Christ is that it is the only way to true freedom to be ourselves—in other words, to become all that we have the potential to be. Obedience frees us from the fetters of Satan. And the truth is that in terms of sheer numbers, it takes greater individuality and courage to follow Christ in this world, "Because strait is the gate, and narrow is the way, which leadeth unto life, and few there be that find it" (Matt. 7:14).

> The great irony of surrendering our will to Christ is that it is the only way to true freedom to be ourselves—to become all that we have the potential to be.

Moreover, in addition to His great plan of salvation for all of His children, Heavenly Father has an individual plan for each of us. He respects and encourages our individuality and wants us to develop it in righteous ways both in this life and in the next. God's own creations testify of His delight in endless variety. "The difference between God and the Devil is that God creates and organizes, while the whole study of the Devil is to destroy" declared Brigham Young (*Discourses of Brigham Young*, John A. Widtsoe, comp. [Salt Lake City: The Church of Jesus Christ of Latter-day Saints, 1977], 69). Thus, the Lord encourages real individuality while Satan obscures it.

May it be our unwavering goal to fill the measure of our unique creation by maintaining our spiritual freedom to explore all of the righteous possibilities God has ordained for us. But we must remember that while there is unlimited variety in almost everything, there is only one way to become the magnificent creatures we are meant to be. That is by surrendering ourselves completely to the empowering arms of Christ.

WHAT CAN THE TEMPLE TEACH ME ABOUT MY ETERNAL IDENTITY?

IT IS NOT POSSIBLE IN this life to completely comprehend who we really were and are and what we may one day become through the Father's plan of salvation and the Savior's Atonement. It is beyond our mortal capacity, though the life of Christ hints at the eternal possibilities. Our memories of the glories and powers of our Heavenly Parents and Their holy realm are blocked out for now, and though we see abundant evidence of Their verity all around us, we must yet exercise faith that They are real and waiting for us. Knowing this would be the case and not wanting us to forget our true identity, our Heavenly Father established the ultimate reminder of where we came from, why we are here, and where we are going—the holy temple. The crown jewel of the gospel and of membership in His earthly kingdom, it affords us a glimpse of our magnificent origins and destiny as we seek to understand its sacred symbols.

> Our memories of our Heavenly Parents and Their holy realm are blocked out for now; we must exercise faith that They are real and waiting for us.

Because our ability to comprehend eternal life is so limited by our mortal bodies and comparatively infant-like spiritual understanding, our Heavenly Father speaks to us through earthly symbols that have many layers of meaning and application. The meaning of a symbol can be both universally understood and specifically applied to an individual at the same time. It can also have different meanings at different times. It can often convey ideas that simply cannot be contained in words. It is the perfect teaching tool.

What can the symbols of the temple tell us about our eternal identity? The answers are as varied as the number of God's children, but here are some of the symbols that are meaningful to us.

Only those who exercise faith in Christ's Atonement and repent of their sins can enter the temple.

There, we are symbolically brought out of the world, cleansed from it, and anointed to one day reign with God in His kingdom. We are also given protection from evil while we are fulfilling our missions on the earth.

We learn that the Lord created the world specifically for us and provided a Savior for us to bring us back to His presence.

We follow in the steps of Adam and Eve. We are just as important to the Lord as they were.

Our exaltation is the Lord's work. He watches over us anxiously and has done everything possible for our salvation.

We progress closer to our eternal destiny as we make and keep covenants.

We are given power, knowledge, and understanding of who we are as we obey.

We learn that Satan is real and desires to destroy us.

We take upon us the name of Christ as we enter into covenants with Him.

We dress in clothing that is symbolic of power, authority, progression, and of our future destiny as kings and queens, priests and priestesses in God's kingdom.

We learn that we are part of a beloved eternal family.

We learn that our destiny is eternal life with our Heavenly Father and Jesus Christ.

The temple itself is symbolic of our heavenly home—the eternal royal palace of our Father—where we were carefully nurtured and prepared for our royal and godly destiny. How fitting, then, that we dress as we do there and receive instruction and training as we do there. No wonder we love to be there, especially when we need to remember who we are, why we are here, and where we are going. It's like going home! The more we attend, the more we learn, the more we apply, the more comfortable we are there, the closer we are to our eternal identity. When we begin to treasure the temple and see it for what it really is, we begin to realize the whole point of our journey through mortality.

The temple with its associated covenants, ordinances, and blessings is the greatest treasure we can take from this life. Our whole quest to reach the temple and find our eternal identity there could be symbolically represented in an insightful story from an apocryphal book, *The Acts of Thomas*, called "Hymn of the Pearl." The Lord revealed to the Prophet Joseph Smith that though there are some falsehoods in the apocrypha, there are also many truths taught that can provide spiritual insight when viewed through the lens of inspiration (see D&C 91:1–5). We think this is one of them. Though not sacred like the teachings of the temple, the symbolism in it speaks louder than words and paints a rich picture of our true identity.

The temple itself is symbolic of our heavenly home, where we were nurtured and prepared for our godly destiny. No wonder we love to be there—it's like going home!

The "Hymn of the Pearl" is the tale of a prince who lived in the heavenly kingdom of his father and mother—the king and queen—and was content with the wealth and luxuries there. But his royal parents had a mission for him. They promised him that if he would go down into "Egypt" (representing the earth) and bring back "the one pearl, which is in the midst of the sea around the loud-breathing serpent," they would make him a joint heir with them and with his brother, who was next to them in authority. They gave him abundantly from their treasury everything he would need to succeed, including a weapon that was very hard and could "crush iron." But in order to accomplish his mission, he had to go in disguise. So he put aside his glorious princely robe and the purple toga that had been woven and prepared just for him and descended into the dangerous world.

"I went straight to the serpent, I dwelt in his abode, [waiting] till he should slumber and sleep, and I could take my pearl from him." At first the prince was faithful in the strange land as he waited for his chance to snatch the pearl. But then he began to interact with the people and to clothe himself in the clothing of the world so they would not find out that he was not one of them and warn the serpent that he had come to take the pearl. Somehow they found out anyway, and instead of confronting him or casting him out, they cleverly began instead to seduce him by giving him their food to eat. This caused him to begin to forget his identity: "I [forgot] that I was a son of kings, and I served their king; and I forgot the pearl, for which my parents had sent me, and because of the burden of their oppressions I lay in a deep sleep."

His heavenly parents were closely watching, however, and were "grieved" for him. They were quick to send a letter reminding him who he was and what he was sent to do. "From thy father, the king of kings, and thy mother, the mistress of the East, and from thy brother, our second [in authority], to thee our son, who art in Egypt, greeting! Call to mind that thou art a son of kings! See the slavery,—whom thou servest! Remember the pearl, for which thou was sent to Egypt! Think of thy robe, and re-member thy splendid toga, which thou shalt wear and (with which) thou shalt be adorned, when thy name hath been read out in the list of the val-iant, and [with] thy brother, our viceroy, thou shalt be in our kingdom."

The king sealed the letter with his own right hand to protect it from evil powers. It took on the form of an eagle and flew directly to the prince. As it landed beside him, it spoke to him. The familiar sound of its voice awakened him from his deep sleep and he grabbed the letter and kissed it. "I began [and] read it; and according to what was traced on my heart were the words of my let-ter. I remembered that I was a son of royal parents, and my noble birth asserted itself. I remembered the pearl, for which I had been sent to Egypt."

By invoking the name of his parents and brother, the second in power, he was able to snatch the pearl away and begin his journey back to his fa-ther's kingdom. With its light and love, the letter also urged him forward as it led him along the path.

As the prince passed on his way toward home with the pearl, trusted mes-sengers from his parents met him. They were bringing his "bright robe" and the toga he had left behind. He marveled greatly at the robe and the toga and how perfectly they fit him and became one with him and "the image of the king of kings was embroidered and depicted in full all over it."

At this point the prince further noticed something remarkable about his royal clothing. It was reflecting his spiritual growth on the earth. As such it was even more beautiful than when he had left it:

> And love urged me to run to meet it and receive it; and I
> stretched forth and took it. With the beauty of its colors I

adorned myself, and I wrapped myself wholly in my toga of brilliant hues. I clothed myself with it, and went up to the gate of salutation and prostration; I bowed my head and worshipped the majesty of my father who sent me,—for I had done his commandments, and he too had done what he promised. . . . (Translations from the Syriac by William Wright, *Apocryphal Acts of the Apostles* [London: Williams and Norgate, 1871], 238–245.)

No Fairy-tale Ending

To most people on earth, the idea that we are princes and princesses and children of God is a fairy tale somewhat like the symbolic tale above. Yet, if we utilize all the tools given to us by our Heavenly Parents before we came to earth and those given continually through the holy prophets while we are on the earth, we will be able to rediscover the secret royal treasures we left behind, retaining a knowledge of who we really were, who we really are, and who we really will be. These powerful tools will enable us to see our fondest dreams come true—not a fairy tale or even a symbolic tale, but what will be the very real eternal destiny of those who remain valiant and faithful:

> **Belief Window**
>
> Do you believe with all your heart that you are truly and literally a son or daughter of a King?

Ye shall come forth in the first resurrection; . . . and shall inherit thrones, kingdoms, principalities, and powers, dominions, all heights and depths . . . and [ye] shall pass by the angels, and the gods, which are set there, to [your] exaltation and glory in all things, as hath been sealed upon [your] heads, which glory shall be a fulness and a continuation of the seeds forever and ever.

Then shall [you] be gods, because [you] have no end; therefore shall [you] be from everlasting to everlasting, because [you] continue; then shall [you] be above all, because all things are subject unto [you]. Then shall [you] be gods, because [you] have all power, and the angels are subject unto [you]. (D&C 132:19–20.)

We began this book by focusing on the ever-growing modern-day crime of identity theft. It is a powerful metaphor for the spiritual crime that has been perpetrated against each one of us by Satan since before the world began. Some of the precautions we can take to prevent our temporal identity from being stolen are also analogous to the basic things we must do to protect our eternal identity.

With temporal identity theft, we must first make sure that our identity is intact. If our identity has been breached or stolen, we must take the necessary steps to restore its integrity. Then we must be constantly vigilant in protecting our identity from those who would gladly steal it and manipulate it for their own selfish purposes.

We must take advantage of the many tools at our disposal to accomplish this. We must carefully heed the warnings given to us about where the threats are coming from and what tactics and schemes are being employed to steal our identity. We must not take chances, be apathetic, or procrastinate but take time-tested steps to protect our valuable identity. Further, we must trust our personal identity information only to those who have proven that they have

> We must guard our eternal identity with our very lives—with all we have and are. We must be able to see the true enemy clearly and keep him far away from us.

our best interests at heart. And finally, we can protect ourselves with insurance that will pay the costs and fix the damage that results if identity theft should occur.

The spiritual parallels to these steps are obvious. If we have forgotten who we are and have fallen short (as we all have; see Rom. 3:23), then the path to regaining our identity is repentance through faith in Jesus Christ and His Atonement. Once our eternal identity is intact and we are on the path to our destiny again, we must guard it with our very lives—with all we have and are. We must be able to see the true enemy clearly and keep him far away from us.

We should not deliberately flirt with danger or even carelessly come too close. We cannot even nibble on the food of worldliness. We gain the power to "crush iron"—to see what is real and to avoid deception and danger as we pray, study, follow the words of scriptures and prophets, heed the promptings of the Holy Ghost, serve others, live worthy of priesthood blessings

We must trust only Jesus Christ with our identity, submitting our will only to Him. Only He can lead us on the path and through the gate back to our Father, King, and God.

and ordinances, participate in the Church, and worship in the temple—all of the simple things the Lord requires of us. Remember that "by small and simple means are great things brought to pass" (Alma 37:6), including exaltation.

Finally, we must trust only Jesus Christ with our identity, submitting our will only to Him. Only He makes it possible to reach the full flower of our potential. Only He insures that the mistakes and messes we make in mortality can be repaired, righted, and erased; our frailties can be overcome and overridden; and our efforts can be productive, pristine, and perfected. Only He can lead us on the path and through the gate back to our Father, King, and God.

"[T]here shall be no other name given nor any other way nor means whereby salvation can come unto the children of men, only in and through the name of Christ, the Lord Omnipotent" (Mosiah 3:17). Only He will never fail us nor forsake us. He is our bright robe, our toga of brilliant hues, our eternal "covering," our all in all. Jesus Christ is our reality.

ABOUT THE AUTHORS

Barbara D. Lockhart is a professor of exercise sciences at Brigham Young University. For many years, she has also taught religion classes at BYU. A convert to the Church, Barbara was taught by the missionaries and baptized while a junior at Michigan State University. She completed her undergraduate and master's degrees at MSU and her doctoral degree at BYU. She competed in several Olympic Games in speed skating for the USA. Prior to teaching at BYU, she taught at Temple University in Philadelphia and at the University of Iowa. She is also a former member of the General Relief Society Board of The Church of Jesus Christ of Latter-day Saints. She is the author of *Cardio Waves: Interval Training for MindBody Wellness.* Barbara was born and raised in Chicago and is the third in a family of four girls.

Wendy C. Top attended Brigham Young University and is the author of *Getting Past the Labels: How the Truth Makes Women Free*. With her husband, Brent, she coauthored *Glimpses Beyond Death's Door*, *Finding Inward Stillness*, and *Finding God in the Garden*. She has served in the Church in many leadership and teaching capacities. Sister Top served as a full-time missionary with her husband when he presided over the Illinois Peoria Mission from 2004 to 2007. She is the mother of four and the grandmother of sixteen.

Brent L. Top is a professor of Church history and doctrine at Brigham Young University and dean of Religious Education. He also served for several years as department chair and associate dean. He has authored or coauthored numerous books, including *What's On the Other Side?*; *LDS Beliefs: A Doctrinal Reference* (with Robert L. Millet, Camille Fronk Olson, and Andrew C. Skinner); *When You Can't Do It Alone*; *The Life Before*; and *The Doctrinal Commentary on the Book of Mormon* (with Robert L. Millet and Joseph Fielding McConkie). He and his wife, Wendy, reside in Pleasant Grove, Utah, where he serves as a stake president.